SURREY

Overdue items may incur charges
as published in the current
Schedule of Charges.

L21

askexplorer.com

Abu Dhabi Top 10 2013/1st Edition
ISBN 978-9948-442-05-9

Front Cover Photograph – Sheikh Zayed Grand Mosque – Pete Maloney

Printed and bound by Emirates Printing Press, Dubai, United Arab Emirates.

Explorer Publishing & Distribution
PO Box 34275, Dubai, United Arab Emirates
Phone   +971 (0)4 340 8805
Fax   +971 (0)4 340 8806
Email   info@askexplorer.com
Web   askexplorer.com

Welcome...

...to **Abu Dhabi Top 10**, your step-by-step guide to the UAE capital. Abu Dhabi is both the UAE's biggest emirate and its capital city – making it a must-see destination for anyone living in or visiting the region.

Whether you're looking for city attractions or outdoor adventures, fine dining or the best beaches, this book is your handy guide to the emirate's essential experiences. In total, we've listed 100 of Abu Dhabi's very best, divided into 10 categories that range from supreme showstopper restaurants to essential family days out, from cracking cultural attractions to the best bars in the city – and plenty more in between. From number one to number 10, they're in no particular order, so make sure you try to get around as many as possible.

And, as we always like to give our readers that little bit extra, you'll also find the top 10 places to visit outside of Abu Dhabi as well as lists of the top 10 malls, 10 not-to-miss golf courses and 10 child-friendly restaurants and cafes that the whole family will love.

So, whether you're visiting Abu Dhabi for a day, a week, a month, or maybe even longer, there's no excuse for not seeing the very best that the city, and the United Arab Emirates, has to offer.

For even more inspiration, **askexplorer.com** is jam-packed with tips for the latest happenings and openings in the UAE and beyond.

Happy exploring,

The Explorer Team

there's more to life...
ask**explorer**.com

GET IN TOUCH WITH
WILDLIFE AND NATURE
AT AL AIN ZOO.

For opening times and special attractions JUST CALL 🕿 800 555
or visit www.alainzoo.ae

  AlAinZooUAE

حديقة الحيوانات بالعين
AL AIN ZOO

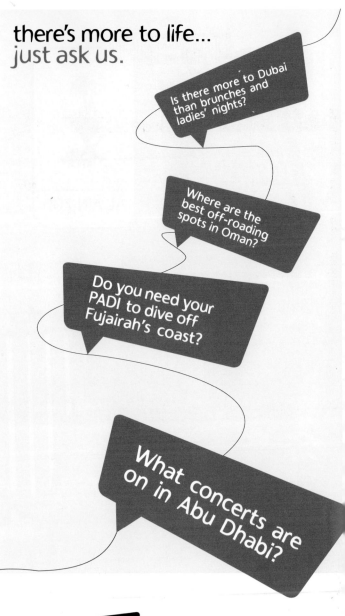

Contents

Welcome To Abu Dhabi 1

Culture & Heritage 1
Modern Abu Dhabi 3
Visiting Abu Dhabi 4
Local Knowledge 4
Media & Further Reading 6
Public Holidays & Annual Events 7
Getting Around 9
Places To Stay 9

askexplorer.com

Since 1996, **explorer** has been the UAE's Number 1 source for all the information you need about living life under the Gulf sun to the fullest.

With some 150 much-loved products in our portfolio, we cover every aspect of life in the Middle East: from off-road adventures to career advice, there's a guide to match all interests – get yours today at **askexplorer.com/shop**.

And for even more insider tips and inspiration, including details of the latest happenings in Dubai, Abu Dhabi and beyond, **askexplorer.com** has all the answers.

Cultural Attractions 13

Heritage Village 16
Al Bateen Boatyard 17
Sheikh Zayed Grand Mosque 18
Al Meena Port 20
Manarat Al Saadiyat 21
Women's Handicraft Centre 22
Folklore Gallery 23
Al Maqtaa Fort 24
The Souk at Qaryat Al Beri 25
Qasr Al Hosn 27

Family Fun 29

Emirates Park Zoo 32
Corniche Road 34
Hili Fun City 36
Abu Dhabi Falcon Hospital 37
Ferrari World 38
Al Ain Zoo 40
Yas Waterworld 41
Wadi Adventure 43
Zayed Sports City 44
Al Forsan 45

Showstopper Restaurants 47

Fishmarket 50
Pachaylen 51
Quest 52
Tiara 54
Mawal 56
Le Deck 57
Marco Pierre White Steakhouse and Grill 58
Ushna 60
Chamas Churrascaria and Bar 61
Mezlai 63

Top 10 Family Restaurants 59

Best Bars 65

Skylite 68
Sho Cho 69
The Beachcomber 70
Impressions 71
Lemon & Lime 74
Left Bank 75
Pearls & Caviar 76
Cloud Nine – Cigar and Champagne Bar 78
Allure by Cipriani 79
Relax@12 81

Shopping Spots 83

Abu Dhabi Mall	87
Souk Al Bawadi	88
The Gold Souk	89
Dalma Mall	90
Khalidiyah Mall	91
Central Market	93
Fish, Fruit & Vegetable Souk	94
Iranian Souk	95
BAS Mall	96
Marina Mall	97

10 Other Malls Not To Miss 93

Destination Hotels 99

Yas Viceroy	103
Emirates Palace	104
Desert Islands Resort & Spa	106
Eastern Mangroves	108
Qasr Al Sarab	110
Sofitel Abu Dhabi Corniche	112
Fairmont Bab Al Bahr	113
Hyatt Capital Gate	114
Shangri-La Qaryat Al Beri	116
Westin Abu Dhabi Golf Resort & Spa	119

Spas 121

Anantara Spa	125
CHI, The Spa	126
Cristal Spa	127
ESPA	129
Zen The Spa	130
Man/Age	131
Zayna Spa	132
Iridium Spa	133
Mizan	134
Hiltonia	135

Adrenaline Activities 137

Hot Air Balloon	140
The Yellow Boats	141
Kayaking	142
Formula Rossa	144
Dune Bashing	145
Kitesurfing	146
Spacewalk	147
Yas Marina Circuit	148
Diving	150
Seawings	152

Places In The Sun 155

On The Water	158
BAKE on Saadiyat Beach	160
Family Park	161
Coast Roads	162
Al Maya Island Resort	164
Fairmont Bab Al Bahr Beach Club	165
The Desert	166
Breakwater	168
Capital Park	169
Monte-Carlo Beach Club	170

Abu Dhabi Experiences 173

The Corniche	176
Desert Safari	178
Friday Brunch	181
Shisha	182
Boat Racing	183
Big Bus Tours	184
Yas Island Weekends	185
Dhow Dinner Cruise	186
Championship Golf Courses	188
Architecture	190

Top 10 Golf Courses 189

Outside Of Abu Dhabi 193

Hatta	196
Oman	197
Dubai	199
Al Ain	202
The Pearl Coast	203
Liwa	205
Fujairah	206
Northern Emirates	207
Emirates National Auto Museum	208
Al Maha Desert Resort & Spa	209

Maps 211

Index 228

View From Jumeirah At Etihad Towers

Welcome To
Abu Dhabi

The thriving cosmopolitan capital in the heart of the Middle East offers architectural splendour, opulent luxury, high-octane thrills and a fascinating heritage.

No longer a sleepy coastal village, the island city of Abu Dhabi is a lush, modern metropolis that has a lot to offer to visitors with its tree-lined streets, futuristic skyscrapers, huge shopping malls and international luxury hotels. The city is surrounded by the sparkling azure waters of the Arabian Gulf, which present a striking contrast to the large parks and green boulevards that spread across the urban island. And, as you'd expect from a truly international destination, there is a wide scope of activities, cuisines and adventures to be found.

Culture & Heritage

Development Of Islam

Islam developed in modern-day Saudi Arabia at the beginning of the seventh century AD with the revelations of the Quran being received by the Prophet Muhammad. Military conquests of the Middle East and North Africa enabled the Arab Empire to spread the teachings of Islam to the local Bedouin tribes. Following the Arab Empire, the Turks, the Mongols and the Ottomans all left their marks on local culture.

The Al Nahyan Family

Despite the opportunities for fishing and grazing, it was not until the discovery of freshwater in 1793 that the ruling Al Nahyan family, based in the south of the country at the Liwa Oasis, moved to Abu Dhabi island. In Liwa, on the edge of the stark Empty Quarter, the Al Nahyan family lived a traditional Bedouin life, with animal husbandry and small-scale agriculture for their livelihood. Descendants of the Al Nahyan family, in alliance with other important Bedouin tribes in the region, have ruled the emirate of Abu Dhabi ever since.

The Trucial States

After the fall of the Muslim empires, both the British and Portuguese became interested in the area due to its strategic position between India and Europe. A series of maritime truces took place, and Abu Dhabi and the other emirates accepted British protection in 1892. In Europe, the area became known as the Trucial Coast (or Trucial States), a name it retained until the departure of the British in 1971.

Independence

In 1968, Britain announced its withdrawal from the region and oversaw the proposed creation of a single state. The ruling sheikhs, particularly of Abu Dhabi and Dubai, realised that by uniting forces they would have a stronger voice in the wider Middle East region. In 1971, the federation of the United Arab Emirates was born.

Formation Of The UAE

The new country comprised the emirates of Dubai, Abu Dhabi, Ajman, Fujairah, Sharjah, Umm Al Quwain and, in 1972, Ras Al Khaimah. The individual emirates each retain a degree of autonomy, with Abu Dhabi and Dubai providing the most input into the federation. The leaders of the new federation elected the ruler of Abu Dhabi, HH Sheikh Zayed bin Sultan Al Nahyan, to be their president, a position he held until he passed away on 2 November 2004. His eldest son,

HH Sheikh Khalifa bin Zayed Al Nahyan, was then elected president.

The Discovery Of Oil
The UAE's formation came after the discovery of huge oil reserves in Abu Dhabi in 1958. The emirate has an incredible 10% of the world's known oil reserves. Exports began four years later, launching Abu Dhabi on its way to incredible wealth.

An Admired Ruler
Sheikh Zayed bin Sultan Al Nahyan was revered by his peers and adored by the public. As UAE president for 33 years and Ruler of Abu Dhabi from 1966 to 2004, he was responsible for many major economic and social advances in Abu Dhabi and across the country, and his vision laid the foundations for today's society.

Culture
Abu Dhabi is a melting pot of nationalities and cultures and the city's effort to become modern and cosmopolitan is proof of an open-minded and liberal outlook. There's a healthy balance between western influences and eastern traditions here.

Food & Drink
Most of the Arabic food available is based on Lebanese cuisine. Common dishes are shawarma (lamb or chicken carved from a spit and served in a pita bread with salad and tahina), falafel (mashed chickpeas and sesame seeds, rolled into balls and deep fried), hummus (a creamy dip made from chickpeas and olive oil), and tabbouleh (finely chopped parsley, mint and crushed wheat).

Among the most famed Middle Eastern delicacies are dates and coffee. Dates are one of the few crops that thrive naturally throughout the Arab world and date palms have been cultivated in the area for around

Traditional wooden dhows have been a central part of Emirati culture for centuries, and it's possible to witness these historical vessels on the Abu Dhabi waterways. At the Al Bateen Boatyard, you can see skilled craftsman still employing traditional techniques and materials to build these stunning ships.

5,000 years. Local coffee is mild with a taste of cardamom and saffron, and it is served black without sugar. Muslims are not allowed to eat pork. In order for a restaurant to have pork on its menu, it should have a separate fridge, preparation equipment and cooking area. Supermarkets are also required to sell pork in a separate area. Alcohol is also considered haram (taboo) in Islam. It is only served in licensed outlets associated with hotels (restaurants and bars), plus a few leisure venues (such as golf clubs) and clubs.

Shisha

Smoking the traditional shisha (water pipe) is a popular and relaxing pastime enjoyed throughout the Middle East. Shisha pipes can be smoked with a variety of aromatic flavours, such as strawberry, grape or apple. Contrary to what many people think, shisha tobacco contains nicotine and can be addictive.

Religion

Islam is the official religion of the UAE and is widely practised; however, there are people of various nationalities and religions working and living in the region side by side.

Muslims are required to pray (facing Mecca) five times a day. Most people pray at a mosque, although it's not unusual to see people kneeling by the side of the road if they are not near a place of worship. The call to prayer, transmitted through loudspeakers on the minarets of each mosque, ensures that everyone knows it's time to pray. Friday is the Islamic holy day, and the first day of the weekend in Abu Dhabi, when most businesses close to allow people to go to the mosque to pray, and to spend time with their families. Many shops and tourist attractions have different hours of operation, opening around 14:00 after Friday prayers.

During the holy month of Ramadan, Muslims abstain from all food, drinks, cigarettes and inappropriate thoughts (or activities) between dawn and dusk for 30 days. In the evening, the fast is broken with the iftar feast. All over the city, festive Ramadan tents are filled to the brim with people of all nationalities and religions enjoying shisha, traditional Arabic mezze and sweets. The timing of Ramadan is not fixed in terms of the Gregorian calendar, but depends on the lunar Islamic calendar.

National Dress

In general, the local population wears traditional dress in public. For men this is the dishdash(a) or khandura: a white full length shirt dress, which is worn with a white or red checked headdress, known as a gutra. This is secured with a black cord (agal). In public, women wear the black abaya – a long, loose robe that covers their normal clothes – plus a headscarf called a sheyla. The abaya is often of sheer, flowing fabric and may be open at the front. Some women also wear a thin black veil hiding their face and/or gloves, and some older women wear a leather mask, known as a burkha, which covers the nose, brow and cheekbones.

Modern Abu Dhabi

People & Economy

The UAE population has grown rapidly in recent years as expat arrivals, robust economic expansion and high birth rates have continued to push up the total number.

According to government statistics, the UAE's population stood at 7.6 million by the end of 2012, with the capital's population estimated at 2.4 million. The UAE Statistics Bureau has, in the past, calculated that the country's population has shot up by as much as 65% over the past five years to reach 8.26 million.

The UAE is among the world's richest countries on a per capita basis. It is the second richest Arab country, after Qatar, thanks to its significant oil wealth. The country has just under 10% of the world's proven oil reserves (most of it within Abu Dhabi). However, successful diversification means that the UAE's wealth is no longer solely reliant on oil revenue.

Tourism

Abu Dhabi was previously viewed by many as Dubai's lesser-known sibling but, in recent years, the capital has set itself up to become a major tourist destination in its own right. Abu Dhabi attracted around 1.8 million visitors in 2010, and with several new hotels and attractions opened, estimates suggest that figure increased to around 2.3 million in 2012.

New Developments

Billions of dirhams are being invested to transform the city into the cultural capital of the Arab world and many key projects focus on art, design and architecture. Yas Island is home to Yas Marina Circuit (home to the Formula 1 Grand Prix), Ferrari World (the world's largest indoor theme park), and Yas Waterworld, with a giant mall soon to join the Yas hotels. The Louvre Abu Dhabi and the Guggenheim Abu Dhabi are due to open over the next few years on Saadiyat Island.

Visiting Abu Dhabi

Getting There

Abu Dhabi International Airport is undergoing a major expansion and redevelopment programme. Terminal 3, exclusively for Etihad flights, opened in 2009 and more additions are on the way.

Airport Transfer

If you book your break through a hotel or travel agency, it's likely that pick-up from the airport will be included. If not, there is a regular bus service between Abu Dhabi International Airport and Abu Dhabi city centre. The fully air-conditioned, green and white bus number 901 runs every 45 minutes, 24 hours a day, from outside the arrivals halls of Terminals 1, 2 and 3. The fare is Dhs.3, however you will need to purchase an Ojra card (ojra.ae).

Visas & Customs

Requirements vary depending on your country of origin and it's wise to check the regulations before departure. GCC nationals (Bahrain,

Kuwait, Qatar, Oman and Saudi Arabia) do not need a visa to enter Abu Dhabi. Citizens from many other countries get an automatic 30-day visa upon arrival at the airport. You can renew this for a further 30 days at a cost of Dhs.620.

Certain medications, including codeine, Temazepam and Prozac, are banned even though they are freely available in other countries

High-profile cases have highlighted the UAE's zero tolerance to drugs. Even a miniscule quantity in your possession could result in a lengthy jail term.

Local Knowledge

Climate

Abu Dhabi has a subtropical and arid climate. Sunny blue skies and high temperatures can be expected most of the year. Rainfall is infrequent, averaging only 25 days per year, mainly in winter (December to March). Summer temperatures can hit a soaring 48°C (118°F) and with humidity well above 60% it can make for uncomfortable conditions from June to September. The most pleasant time to visit Abu Dhabi is during winter when average temperatures range between 14°C and 30°C.

Time

The UAE is four hours ahead of UTC (Universal Coordinated Time – formerly known as GMT). There is no altering of clocks for daylight saving in the summer. Most offices and schools are closed during the weekend, on Fridays and Saturdays. Be aware that the Metro and some shops don't open until later on Fridays.

Electricity & Water

The electricity supply is 220/240 volts and 50 cycles. Most hotel rooms and villas use the three-pin plug that is used in the UK. Adaptors are widely available and only cost a few dirhams. Tap water is desalinated sea water and is perfectly safe to drink although most people choose mineral water because it tastes better and is cheap.

Sheikh Zayed Grand Mosque

Ferrari World

Abu Dhabi provides a fascinating mix of the old and the new. While the emirate is careful to preserve the traditions and culture of the past, it is also home to awe-inspiring modern architecture and record-breaking theme parks.

Abu Dhabi Golf Club

Credit Cards & Cash

Credit and debit cards are widely accepted around Abu Dhabi. Foreign currencies and travellers' cheques can be exchanged in licensed exchange offices, banks and hotels. Cash is preferred in the souks, markets and in smaller shops, and paying in cash will help your bargaining power. If you've hired a car, be aware that only cash is accepted at petrol pumps.

The monetary unit is the dirham (Dhs.), which is divided into 100 fils. The currency is also referred to as AED (Arab Emirate Dirham). Notes come in denominations of Dhs.5 (brown), Dhs.10 (green), Dhs.20 (light blue), Dhs.50 (purple), Dhs.100 (pink), Dhs.200 (yellowy-brown), Dhs.500 (blue) and Dhs.1,000 (browny-purple). The dirham has been pegged to the US dollar since 1980, at a mid rate of $1 to Dhs.3.6725.

Language

Arabic is the official language of the UAE, although English, Hindi, Malayalam and Urdu are commonly spoken. You can easily get by with English, but you're likely to receive at least a smile if you can throw in a couple of Arabic words.

Crime & Safety

Pickpocketing and crimes against tourists are a rarity in Abu Dhabi, and visitors can enjoy feeling safe and unthreatened in most places around the city. Abu Dhabi Police will advise you on a course of action in the case of a loss or theft. If you've lost something in a taxi, call the taxi company. If you lose your passport, your next stop should be your embassy or consulate. If you are crossing the road on foot, use designated pedestrian crossings (jaywalking is illegal) and, if you plan on driving, make sure you know the rules of the road. There is zero tolerance towards drink driving, even after one pint, and if you're caught you can expect a spell in prison.

Accidents & Emergencies

If you witness an accident or need an ambulance in an emergency situation, the number to call is 999. For urgent medical care, there are several private hospitals with excellent A&E facilities. With the exception of emergency care in government hospitals, which is available for free unless you require any follow-up treatment, you will need a health card to access government health services. For general non-emergency medical care, most hospitals have a walk-in clinic where you can simply turn up.

People With Disabilities

Abu Dhabi is starting to consider the needs of visitors with special needs more seriously although, in general, facilities remain somewhat limited, particularly at older attractions. Most of Abu Dhabi's five-star hotels have wheelchair facilities and Abu Dhabi International Airport is well equipped for physically challenged travellers. There is a special check-in gate with direct access from the car park, as well as dedicated lifts, and a meet and assist service.

Mobile & Internet

It is possible to buy temporary (three-month) SIM cards for mobile phones that work on a pay-as-you go basis. Etisalat's 'Ahlan' package costs Dhs.60, including Dhs.25 credit and lasts 90 days. du's pre-paid package costs Dhs.55 with a welcome bonus of Dhs.10, usage bonus of Dhs.100, and lifetime validity (provided minimum top-ups are made). You can easily buy top-up cards for both packages from supermarkets, newsagents and petrol stations. Wi-Fi is available in many hotels and cafes around town.

Media & Further Reading

Many of the major glossy magazines are available in Abu Dhabi, but if they're imported from the US or Europe, you can expect to pay at least twice the normal cover price. Alternatively, you can pick up the Middle East versions of popular titles including Harper's Bazaar, Grazia, OK! and Hello, where you'll find all the

Abu Dhabi's spectacular Corniche is the social hub of the city. It stretches for seven kilometres alongside the sparkling azure waters of the Arabian Gulf, providing the perfect place for a leisurely stroll. It is also home to some of the best dining options in the emirate, as well as parks and gardens.

English language stations operate 24 hours a day and, while most are physically based in Dubai, they can usually be picked up with good reception throughout Abu Dhabi: Emirates Radio 1 (100.5FM & 104.1FM) and 2 (99.3FM), Dubai 92 (92.0FM), Channel 4 (104.8FM), Virgin Radio (104.4FM) and The Coast (103.2FM).

Public Holidays & Annual Events

regular gossip and news, with extras from around the region. All international titles are examined and, where necessary, censored to ensure that they don't offend the country's moral codes.

Television
Most hotels have satellite or cable, broadcasting a mix of local and international channels. You'll find MTV, major news stations and some BBC programming, in addition to the standard hotel info loop. The local television channels in Abu Dhabi are rapidly improving and they often show episodes of US talk shows and popular sitcoms.

Radio
Catering for Abu Dhabi's multinational inhabitants, there are stations broadcasting in English, French, Hindi, Malayalam and Urdu. The leading

Public Holidays
The Islamic calendar starts from the year 622AD, the year of Prophet Muhammad's migration (Hijra) from Mecca to Al Madinah. Hence, the Islamic year is called the Hijri year and dates are followed by AH (AH stands for Anno Hegirae, meaning 'after the year of the Hijra'). As some holidays are based on the sighting of the moon and do not have fixed dates on the Hijri calendar, Islamic holidays are more often than not confirmed less than 24 hours in advance. The main Muslim festivals are Eid Al Fitr (the festival of the breaking of the fast, which marks the end of Ramadan) and Eid Al Adha (the festival of the sacrifice, which marks the end of the pilgrimage to Mecca). Mawlid Al Nabee is the holiday celebrating Prophet Muhammad's birthday, and Lailat Al Mi'raj celebrates the Prophet's ascension into heaven.

In general, public holidays are unlikely to disrupt your visit to Abu Dhabi except that shops may open a bit later and, on a few specific days, alcohol is not served.

Annual Events

Abu Dhabi hosts an impressive array of events, from Formula 1 racing and international tennis to well-respected music and film festivals. Many attract thousands of visitors, and tickets often sell out quickly.

Dhow Racing
All year round
adimsc.ae
Scheduled dhow races take place throughout the year, mostly between October and April.

Abu Dhabi HSBC Golf Championship
January
abudhabigolfchampionship.com
There's over $2 million in prize money up for grabs, and some of the biggest names in world golf take part.

Abu Dhabi Festival
March
abudhabifestival.ae
Brings big names in classical music and fine arts to the capital every year, with past performers including Bolshoi Ballet, Andrea Bocelli, Sir James Galway and Yo-Yo Ma.

Abu Dhabi Desert Challenge
April
abudhabidesertchallenge.ae
The event attracts some of the world's top rally drivers and bike riders who compete in the car, truck and motocross categories over four days.

Al Gharbia Watersports Festival
April
algharbiafestivals.com
From kiteboards and surf ski kayaks among the waves to chilled-out camping and concerts, this 10-day watersports extravaganza has it all for the UAE's beach lovers. The on-shore entertainment also includes beach football and volleyball.

WOMAD Abu Dhabi
April
womadabudhabi.ae
Co-founded by Peter Gabriel, the local edition of the World of Music, Arts and Dance festival is a three-day affair that attracts nearly 100,000 spectators.

Powerboat Racing
October to May
adimsc.ae
Abu Dhabi International Marine Sports Club hosts races from October to May, including the final round of the season. These events include the F1 Powerboat World Championships, which uses similar rules and regulations to F1 car races.

WOMAD Abu Dhabi

Al Ain Aerobatic Show

November-December
alainaerobaticshow.com
The five-day show features flying
daredevils from all over the world
displaying their incredible aerial skills
with a host of aerobatic stunts.

Abu Dhabi Film Festival

November
abudhabifilmfestival.ae
This festival has gone from strength to
strength to become one of the
region's premier film events. Previous
star-studded editions have been
attended by the likes of Cate
Blanchett, Uma Thurman, Clive Owen,
Tilda Swinton and Richard Gere.

Formula 1 Etihad Airways Abu Dhabi Grand Prix

November
formula1.com
As it is one of the last races of the F1
season, excitement is always
guaranteed on the track, while the
event also features a number of big
name entertainers performing on
stage at the end of each day.

Mubadala World Tennis Championship

December
mubadalawtc.com
After a few years of hosting the
world's top male players (Federer,
Nadal, Murray, Djokovic) and
attracting record crowds of up to
15,000 fans, this tournament has
quickly become the hottest end-of-
year sporting ticket.

Getting Around

Bus

There are dozens of bus routes
servicing the main residential and
commercial areas of Abu Dhabi. The
buses and bus shelters are air-
conditioned, modern and clean,
services run more or less around the
clock, and fares are inexpensive (as
little as Dhs.2 for travel within the
capital). The main bus station is on
Hazza bin Zayed Road and there are
bus stops in many of the main
residential districts. 'Ojra' bus passes

can be purchased at the central bus
station or at any Red Crescent kiosk
on the island, and an inter-urban pass
costs Dhs.80 for one month of
unlimited use. The front three rows of
seats on all buses are reserved for
women and children only.
Visit ojra.ae for downloadable bus
route maps.

Driving & Car Hire

Driving is on the right hand side,
wearing seat belts is mandatory in the
front seats, and speed limits are
usually around 60 to 80kmph in town,
and 100 to 120kmph on major roads.
These are strictly enforced by cameras.
    You will find all the major car rental
companies in Abu Dhabi, plus a few
local ones. It is best to shop around as
rates can vary considerably.

Taxi

Taxis are reasonably priced, plentiful
and the most common method of
getting around. The city has a 7,000-
strong taxi fleet overseen by TransAD
(transad.ae). Most trips around the city
shouldn't cost more than Dhs.15.
Daytime (06:00-22:00) metered fares
in the city start at Dhs.3.5; nighttime
fares are slightly more, with the
starting fare at Dhs.4 and a minimal
fare of Dhs.10 after 22:00.

Walking & Cycling

Most cities in the UAE are very
car-oriented and not designed to
encourage walking. Additionally,
summer temperatures of more than
45°C are not conducive to a leisurely
stroll. Having said that, the relative
compactness of Abu Dhabi's main
area makes walking and cycling a
pleasant way of getting around in
the cooler winter months, and an
evening stroll or bike ride along the
Corniche is a must.

Places To Stay

The standard of accommodation in
the emirate is so high that once
you've spent a night or two in an Abu
Dhabi five-star hotel, you might find
five-star hotels in other parts of the
world a bit disappointing.

Most of Abu Dhabi's traditional hotels are on the northern end of the island, near the Corniche, but following the opening of several venues in areas such as Al Maqtaa and Yas Island, visitors now have a wide range of choice.

Al Maqta Hotel
02 617 0000
Map p.219

Al Raha Beach Hotel
danathotels.com
02 508 0555
Map p.221

Aloft Abu Dhabi
aloftabudhabi.com
02 654 5000
Map p.218

Crowne Plaza Yas Island
ichotelsgroup.com
02 656 3000
Map p.224

Eastern Mangroves Hotel & Spa By Anantara
anantara.com
02 656 1000
Map p.217

Emirates Palace
kempinski.com
02 690 9000
Map p.214

Fairmont Bab Al Bahr
fairmont.com
02 654 3333
Map p.219

Hilton Abu Dhabi
hilton.com
02 681 1900
Map p.214

Hyatt Capital Gate Abu Dhabi
hyatt.com
02 596 1234
Map p.218

InterContinental Abu Dhabi
ichotelsgroup.com
02 666 6888
Map p.214

Jumeirah At Etihad Towers
jumeirah.com
02 811 5555
Map p.214

One To One Hotel – The Village
onetoonehotels.com
02 495 2000
Map p.216

Park Hyatt Abu Dhabi Hotel & Villas
hyatt.com
02 407 1234
Map p.227

The Ritz-Carlton Grand Canal
ritzcarlton.com
02 818 8888
Map p.219

Shangri-La Hotel, Qaryat Al Beri
shangri-la.com
02 509 8888
Map p.219

The St Regis Saadiyat Island Resort
stregissaadiyatisland.com
02 498 8888
Map p.227

The Westin Abu Dhabi Golf Resort & Spa
westinabudhabigolfresort.com
02 616 9999
Map p.220

Yas Viceroy Abu Dhabi
viceroyhotelsandresorts.com
02 656 0000
Map p.224

Desert Escapes
Located a few hours west of the city, the region known as Al Gharbia boasts stunning scenery.

Desert Islands Resort & Spa By Anantara
desertislands.anantara.com
02 801 5400
Map p.212

Qasr Al Sarab Desert Resort By Anantara
anantara.com
02 886 2088
Map p.212

Monte-Carlo Beach Club

Despite its growing modern developments, from luxury resorts to record-breaking theme parks, Abu Dhabi has maintained strong links to its history. Within the emirate it is still possible to see reminders of centuries-old pastimes, from dhows and fortresses to traditional Islamic architecture.

Yas Viceroy

Fairmont Bab Al Bahr

Whenever you
read a good book,
somewhere in the world
a door opens to allow
in more light

**JASHANMAL
BOOKSTORES**

Cultural
Attractions

Heritage Village 16

Al Bateen Boatyard 17

Sheikh Zayed Grand Mosque 18

Al Meena Port 20

Manarat Al Saadiyat 21

Women's Handicraft Centre 22

Folklore Gallery 23

Al Maqtaa Fort 24

The Souk at Qaryat Al Beri 25

Qasr Al Hosn 27

Traditional Dhows

Cultural
Attractions
Introduction

Abu Dhabi is teeming with fascinating places to visit, many of which offer glimpses into a time when the city and emirate was nothing more than a small trading post and an endless desert.

Abu Dhabi achieves what a large number of Middle Eastern cities fail to realise: a healthy balance between western influences and eastern traditions. While the emirate is very much looking to the future, it is also very much rooted in the Islamic customs that deeply penetrate the Arabian Peninsula and beyond.

The UAE's successful effort to become modern and cosmopolitan is proof of an open-minded and liberal outlook. Consequently, the rapid economic development over the last 30 years has changed life in the emirate beyond recognition. Yet the country's rulers are committed

Ramadan Timings

During the Islamic holy month of Ramadan, Muslims fast from sunrise to sunset for 30 days. The exact dates of Ramadan change every year due to the fact that Islam uses a lunar calendar (each month begins with the sighting of a new moon). As a result, Islamic holidays begin on different days with Ramadan taking place 11 days earlier each year according to the western Gregorian calendar. It is worth checking when you will be visiting Abu Dhabi as, during Ramadan, timings for many companies change significantly. Museums and heritage sites, for instance, usually open slightly later in the morning than usual, and close earlier in the afternoon.

to safeguarding their heritage, and have gone to huge lengths to promote cultural and sporting events that are representative of the region's traditions. Falconry, camel racing and traditional dhow sailing are all popular, as is Arabic poetry, dancing, songs and traditional art and craftsmanship. Courtesy and hospitality are the most highly-prized virtues, and visitors are likely to experience the genuine warmth and friendliness of the Emirati people during their stay.

Abu Dhabi features many fascinating places to visit, each of which offers a glimpse into a time when the city was nothing more than a small trading port and centre for pearl diving. Many of the pre-oil heritage sites have been carefully restored, paying close attention to authentic design and using original building materials. Stroll through the Heritage Village, with its traditional-style huts and homes, and marvel at how people coped in Abu Dhabi long before air-conditioning.

The Sheikh Zayed Grand Mosque offers fascinating insights into local culture and its links to religion, while there are numerous galleries that have interesting exhibitions of art and traditional Arabic artefacts, and more are springing up all the time.

Meanwhile, the Louvre Abu Dhabi, Guggenheim Abu Dhabi and Zayed National Museum are currently being constructed on Saadiyat Island.

Heritage Village

Location Breakwater **Web** torath.ae
Times 09:00-17:00 daily, 15:30-21:00 Fridays
Map 1 p.215

The picture postcard Heritage Village is located on the Breakwater near Marina Mall, and, facing back towards Abu Dhabi's Corniche and waterfront, the cityscape view alone is almost worth the visit. But the Heritage Village is a fascinating addition to any tourist's itinerary.

The little spice shop is a real treat; you can get a range of dried herbs and even handmade soap. It's a great place to buy the expensive spice saffron for far less than in major supermarkets.

Run by the Emirates Heritage Club, it offers an interesting glimpse into the country's past. Traditional aspects of the Bedouin way of desert life, including a camp fire with coffee pots, a goats' hair tent, a well and a falaj irrigation system, are displayed in the open museum. Meanwhile, there are workshops where craftsmen demonstrate traditional skills, such as metalwork and pottery, while women sit weaving and spinning. The craftsmen are happy to share their skills and may occasionally give you the chance to try them out. After visiting the village, sample some Arabic cuisine at the neighbouring waterside restaurants.

Al Bateen Boatyard

Location Al Bateen, close to the InterContinental hotel
Times Daily, except Fridays
Map 2 p.215

The Al Bateen area, on the western side of Abu Dhabi, stretches along the coast between the InterContinental hotel and 19th Street. One of the capital's most affluent areas, with plenty of green, open spaces, it has a pleasant, residential neighbourhood feel that is worlds away from the nearby city centre.

The highlight of the area is the Al Bateen Boatyard. It's here that you'll find the craftsmen who employ traditional skills to build the dhows and racing hulls that can be seen in competitions off the Corniche. The method they use has changed little over the centuries and each dhow is still a testament to the patience, technique and love of its creator. As you approach the boatyard, you'll be taken in by the evocative smells of freshly cut African and Indian teak and, if it's not too busy, the craftsmen will happily share the intricacies of their art and may even let you try your hand at dhow building. The yard is open every day except Friday and the best time to visit is around 17:00.

Be warned that this area is currently changing as the whole marina is being redeveloped to create the new Al Bateen Wharf. Although being developed in phases, what's open one week may not be there the next.

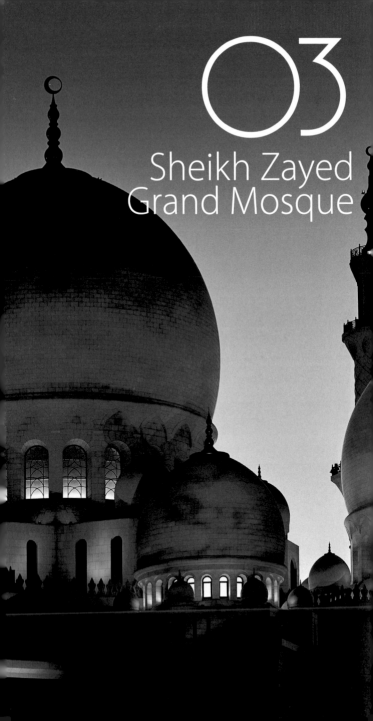

03

Sheikh Zayed Grand Mosque

Location Al Maqtaa, Abu Dhabi **Web** szgmc.ae
Tel 02 441 6444 **Times** 09:00-22:00 (Saturday to Thursday),
closed Friday mornings
Price Guide Free **Map** 3 p.219

The stunning Sheikh Zayed Grand Mosque opened in 2007 and has captivated worshippers and visitors since. This work of art is the largest mosque in the UAE and one of the largest in the world, with a capacity for an astonishing 40,000 worshippers, which it often sees during Eid.

The Grand Mosque dominates arrival onto the island via the Al Maqtaa, Mussafah and Sheikh Zayed bridges, towering over the south of the island and so pristine and white that is appears to almost shimmer underneath the blue skies.

The mosque's first event was the funeral of its namesake, Sheikh Zayed, who is buried at the site.

Architecturally, the mosque was inspired by Mughal and Moorish traditions, with classical minarets. The most amazing features are perhaps the 80 domes, more than 1,000 columns, 24-carat gold chandeliers, or the world's largest hand-woven Persian carpet, which was designed by a renowned Iranian artist. If the effect is breathtaking during the day, then words can barely describe the vision that is the Grand Mosque illuminated at night.

Unlike other mosques, Sheikh Zayed Mosque is open for non-Muslims to tour between 09:00 and 22:00 every day except for Friday mornings, although you might like to time your visit to coincide with one of the free 'walk in' guided tours that take place at 10:00, 11:00 and 16:30 during the week, at 16:30 and 20:00 on Friday, and at 10:00, 11:00, 14:00, 16:30 and 20:00 on Saturday. You will learn more about not only the mosque but Islam in general.

Remember to dress conservatively if you plan to visit the Grand Mosque. Men should avoid wearing shorts or short sleeves, while women should wear loose-fitting clothes that cover legs and shoulders. Shawls are provided at the entrance for ladies to cover their heads.

04
Al Meena Port

Location Northeastern tip of Abu Dhabi island
Map 4 p.226

The Al Meena port area is an excellent destination for visitors. Located on the north-eastern tip of the island, this is where you'll find Port Zayed, which is known for its working port, dhow harbour and souks.

This port is home to the fish, fruit and vegetable market, a carpet souk and the Iranian souk, which is an odd market-like collection of stores selling all sorts of bizarre knick-knacks. The Iranian traders come over on their dhows every three weeks or so – sometimes you'll be lucky and catch a new consignment of intricately-detailed pots and plates; other times there'll be no one around. These souks

offer an entirely different shopping experience to the malls: here, you can practise your bartering skills and walk away with a bargain.

The dhow harbour, off Port Road, is a contrast of past and present with several hundred dhows resting in their berths. Much like Al Bateen (p.17), it is a fascinating place to explore early in the morning when the fishermen return from sea. Try out the nearby restaurants, which offer an authentic selection of local cooking – grilled meats and seafood. The harbour is also worth a visit at sunset when the dhows return, particularly if you're a keen photgrapher.

Manarat Al Saadiyat

Location Saadiyat Island **Web** saadiyatculturaldistrict.ae
Tel 02 657 5800 **Times** 09:00-20:00
Price Guide Free **Map** 5 p.227

There are, of course, huge amounts of excitement and enthusiasm for the cultural developments taking place on Saadiyat Island as completion dates draw nearer and nearer. Within a couple of years, visitors to the 'island of happiness' will be able to spend the morning in the Frank Gehry-designed Guggenheim Abu Dhabi, before spending a few hours in the Louvre Abu Dhabi (Jean Nouvel is the architect of that building), and finishing off the day in the Zayed National Museum, to be housed in an incredible Sir Norman Foster structure.

To find out more about the epic forthcoming cultural offerings of Saadiyat, including the Guggenheim Abu Dhabi, the Louvre Abu Dhabi, and the Zayed National Museum,

head to Manarat Al Saadiyat. As well as being home to an interactive exhibition about the changing face of Saadiyat, it is also a cultural venue in its own right.

Manarat Al Saadiyat is part exhibition space and part Saadiyat visitor centre – a 15,400 square metre space where you'll find the Arts Abu Dhabi Gallery, the Contemporary Art Gallery and the Universal Art Gallery. A number of temporary exhibitions, showcasing works from some of the biggest names in modern art, have already passed through Manarat Al Saadiyat.

In addition, there are several galleries and auditoriums, as well as a 250-seat theatre, and the excellent Fanr restaurant.

© Abu Dhabi Tourism & Culture Authority

Women's Handicraft Centre

Location Karama St, Al Mushrif **Web** visitabudhabi.ae
Tel 02 447 6645 **Times** 09:00-22:00 (Sunday to Thursday)
Price Guide Dhs.5 per person **Map** 6 p.216

The Women's Handicraft Centre is a creative and artistic initiative to showcase local art, crafts and traditional practices. Sponsored by the Abu Dhabi Government and run by the Abu Dhabi Women's Association, the first point of call is the museum which, although on the small side, does provide some interesting examples of traditional local weaving, costume making and camel bags, along with some information on the crafts.

However, the small round huts at the back of the museum are what you really come here to see. Inside each, you'll find groups of Emirati women chatting and practising the traditional crafts of saddu, talli, textile weaving, embroidering,

tailoring, basket-weaving, palm-tree frond weaving, and henna. These crafts have been practised by women and passed down through the generations; at the Women's Handicraft Centre, the women are continuing this proud tradition. Remember to remove your shoes before entering a hut and to ask permission before taking photos; and your pics should focus on the crafts rather than the women themselves. Male visitors should not get too close to the women.

Female visitors can experience the ancient art of henna, with a small hand design (that will last a couple of weeks) costing just Dhs.10. The onsite shop is also an excellent place to pick up some authentic keepsakes.

Folklore Gallery

Location Shk Zayed The First St, Al Khalidiyah **Web** folkloregallery.net
Tel 02 666 0361 **Times** 09:00-22:00 (Saturday to Thursday)
Price Guide Free **Map** **7** p.215

Abu Dhabi is setting itself up as the Middle East's art hub, and it's important to remember that, while giant mega-galleries are being constructed on Saadiyat Island (p.21) there are also plenty of excellent small galleries already scattered throughout the city. The pick of the crop, arguably, is the Folklore Gallery, which has been open since 1995.

Ostensibly a framing gallery, it's still the best place to have artwork professionally framed or mounted. However, such is the passion for art, the gallery has become a lot more than that. The gallery showcases paintings, drawings and sculptures by its roster of resident artists. These items are all affordable entries into the world of art.

The Abu Dhabi Art Fair is a four-day event held every November at Emirates Palace Ballroom, showcasing work from 50 galleries in 19 countries. Previous artists have included de Kooning, Rochter and Basquiat.

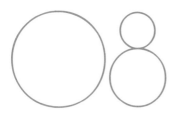

Al Maqtaa Fort

Location Nr Al Maqtaa Bridge, Al Maqtaa
Web visitabudhabi.ae
Map 8 p.219

This heavily renovated fort is one of the few remaining examples of its kind in Abu Dhabi city, and provides a wonderful contrast to the modern bridge right next to it. Your best view of Al Maqtaa Fort is likely to be on the approach to Abu Dhabi island, just before crossing one of the bridges.

Standing on the edge of the island, this 200-year-old fort is a reminder of times gone by, when its principal purpose was to protect Abu Dhabi from the bandits who prowled along the waterways.

Unfortunately, one of Abu Dhabi's most iconic and symbolic buildings cannot be directly accessed as it stands in a sensitive military zone and, therefore, remains closed to the public. Be careful when trying to photograph the fort as there are regular police patrols.

The Souk
at Qaryat Al Beri

Location Qaryat Al Beri Complex
Times 10:00-22:00 weekdays, 10:00-23:00 weekends, 15:00-23:00 Fridays **Map** 9 p.219

The centre point of the Qaryat Al Beri complex – which lies between the Al Maqtaa and Mussafah bridges on the mainland, looking over the island and the Sheikh Zayed Grand Mosque – the Souk at Qaryat Al Beri is a contemporary adaptation of a typical souk.

Built over two levels, the complex is a fusion of age-old Arabian architecture with a Venetian theme, romantic canals and lush gardens snaking their way through the souk and connecting it to the Shangri-la and Traders hotels.

The souk is a rabbit's warren of outlets, which are predominantly aimed at tourists and, as such, are maybe a little pricier than you'll find elsewhere. But, for the experience and atmosphere alone, the extra couple of dirhams are worth paying. Look out for dates, chocolates and a handful of cheesy camel-themed souvenirs as well as niche items, such as antiques, and heritage pieces.

The real reason for the Souk at Qaryat Al Beri's increasing popularity, however, is its extensive and diverse collection of cafes, bars and restaurants. Almost all offer alfresco dining with views over the creek. Hop on one of the tourist dhows that sail the waterways for a different perspective of the souk.

Qasr Al Hosn

Location Markaziya West
Web en.qasralhosnfestival.ae
Map 10 p.215

Surrounded on all four sides by towers that house apartments, offices and stores, this large city block is perhaps the last place that you'd expect to find one of the most venerable slices of traditional Abu Dhabi life. However, wedged in between Old Airport Road, Al Nasr Street and Electra Street, just a few roads back from the Corniche, is exactly where you'll find Qasr Al Hosn.

Often referred to as The Old Fort or The White Fort, whatever you call it, Qasr Al Hosn is the city's oldest surviving building, dating back to 1793. For decades, it was the official residence of the rulers of Abu Dhabi when they made the move from the Liwa Oasis to the island; from here, the sheikhs of Al Nahyan defended the island up until 1966.

Along with the neighbouring Cultural Foundation – an amazing labyrinth of arts, culture, crafts and creativity that contains a library and theatre as well as classrooms and exhibition spaces – Qasr Al Hosn was Abu Dhabi's main cultural attraction until it closed for major renovation a few years ago. However, the area will open again soon as a heritage museum and public monument.

Qasr Al Hosn temporarily reopened in February for an annual 10-day festival celebrating more than 250 years as a fort. This included the *Story of a Fort, Legacy of a Nation* show by Franco Dragone, best known for directing Le Reve.

Family Fun

Emirates Park Zoo 32

Corniche Road 34

Hili Fun City 36

Abu Dhabi Falcon Hospital 37

Ferrari World 38

Al Ain Zoo 40

Yas Waterworld 41

Wadi Adventure 43

Zayed Sports City 44

Al Forsan 45

Wadi Adventure

Family Fun
Introduction

Much of Abu Dhabi's appeal lies in the fact that it is truly a destination with something for everyone, and there are some stunning attractions that cater for the whole family.

Family plays a huge part in Abu Dhabi life, as well as being integral to Emirati culture and, no matter where you go, children are rarely expected to be seen and not heard. Many restaurants are abuzz with kids running around and there are numerous weekend brunches aimed specifically at families, with entertainment such as face painting, bouncy castles, art classes and games all laid on to help the younger family members enjoy the day every bit as much as mum and dad.

As well as some of the more individual family attractions listed in this chapter, the biggest malls in town provide bounteous destinations when it comes to keeping kids entertained. The majority have some sort of entertainment centre or games areas, while others have extra special attractions, such as the mini skating rink at Marina Mall and the splash park at Mushrif Mall. Cinemas also have a pretty open door policy, although you'd do well to respect the recommended age restrictions, as much out of consideration for other patrons as for the enjoyment of your children.

During the cooler months, Abu Dhabi's parks are great family locations, and you'll find everything from children's play areas with climbing frames, swings and slides to kiosks renting out bikes and pedal-powered go-karts, which are permanent fixtures at many of the largest parks. The beach parks along the Corniche are positively packed with activities to keep young ones entertained. And you'll likely find an ice cream stand or two to boot, of course, as well as other food stalls for grabbing a quick bite to eat.

If you're staying at one of Abu Dhabi's bigger resorts, the children may not ever want to leave the hotel, such is the range of activities available, from kids' clubs to swimming pools, and beaches to watersports. If your hotel doesn't have a kids' club, some locations, such as Monte-Carlo Beach Club (p.170), run children's clubs.

If your hotel doesn't have a pool, then, other than the amazing waterpark on Yas Island (p.41), hitting the beach is really the only option as public pools outside of hotels and sports clubs are rare in Abu Dhabi. One good option would be to get a day pass at one of the bigger resort hotels, giving you access to the pool and facilities for a full day. Some of the resorts, such as Hiltonia, offer watersports; many of these aquatic thrills, including donutting and banana boat riding, are also suitable activities for teens.

A word of caution while out and about by the beach: it is unwise to let your children swim in the sea unsupervised, especially at the public beaches, as there can sometimes be strong undercurrents.

Choosing Hotels

Check out what activities come included with your hotel booking before making a reservation. Some of the Yas Island hotels, for example, offer fantastic multi-activity packages that include family entry to Ferrari World and Yas Waterworld or even rounds of golf.

Emirates Park Zoo

Location Al Bahya **Web** emiratesparkzoo.com
Tel 02 563 3100 **Times** 9:30-20:00 (Sunday to Wednesday), 9:30-21:00
(Thursday to Saturday and Public Holidays) **Price Guide** Dhs.20 (Adult),
Dhs.5 (Under 6), free (Under 2) **Map** **1** p.211

The Emirates Park Zoo, which is a 30-minute drive or so outside of downtown Abu Dhabi, has recently seen some major renovations and is now one of the best and most popular kids' attractions in the emirate – although mum and day should enjoy visiting too.

The aim of the zoo is to give children the chance to get up close to their favourite animals, in order to combine learning about nature with touch and interaction. Wild attractions at the zoo include a bird park, a flamingo park, the 'Giraffe Cafe', an ocean park, the predator and primate sections, and the scary-sounding snake alley. There are, in total, more than 2,000 species on display, including camels, wallabies, pelicans, zebras, eels, clownfish, white tigers, brown bears, blue monkeys, chameleons and pythons. Anacondas, hippos and sea lions are on the way.

The highlight of a day at the Emirates Park Zoo has to be feeding the giraffes and zebras in the 'Giraffe Cafe', or bottlefeeding free-roaming lambs and goats in the Children's Farm area. Bunches of grass and carrots cost from Dhs.5.

The perfect place for an avid lover of the Middle East holiday is located on the Abu Dhabi - Dubai highway, 30 minutes away from Abu Dhabi.

Only two minutes from Formula F1 assembly point, The best thing about our Zoo is interacting with many kind of 1700 animals inside the Zoo, to complete this unique experience we available an 60 sq meter chalet with direct and indirect view to the zoo, So let your holiday experience be a unique one as you enjoy the beauty in the company of wild animals. Everyone has a chance for a realistic experience to closely watch these animals.

In a hectic lifestyle for people who strive to break free, we think it's pretty good option to see that you take a chance for the holidays. If you are a parent of young kids, we are sure you will share an almost different desire to make your holidays a special one for your families. They need not be costly, but it should be enjoyable and connect with your family's mood.

A day spent at Emirates Park zoo & Resort, will give you a whole new definition about a convenient and relaxed stay. Our blend of superior accommodations, services, modern amenities and lively atmosphere is what you will take home after leaving us, we guarantee that.

phone: +971 2 563 31 00 • **fax:** +971 2 563 12 66 • www.emiratesparkzoo.com • الباهية، أبوظبي، الإمارات العربية المتحدة
phone: +971 2 563 31 00 • **fax:** +971 2 563 12 66 • www.emiratesparkzoo.com • Al Bahia, Abu Dhabi - UAE

02
Corniche
Road

Corniche Road boasts an impressive six kilometres of parks that include children's play areas, separate cycle and pedestrian paths, cafes and restaurants, and Corniche Beach, a life-guarded beach park.

There is the Family Park near King Khalid bin Abdul Aziz Street (26th Street), with its creative play areas for toddlers and older kids, a cafe, and BBQ and picnic areas; the Urban Park near Sheikh Rashid bin Saeed Al Maktoum Street, with its beautiful garden; the Lake Park near Muroor Street, known for its 'lake'; and the Formal Park by Baniyas Street, noted for its architecture and maze. There is plenty of parking on the city side of Corniche Road, and pedestrian underpasses at all the major intersections connect to the waterfront side.

These parks are very popular among city folk, especially during weekends, as families take a stroll, have picnics and get-togethers, or simply burn off some energy.

Bikes and pedal cars are for hire in the various parks and along the Corniche at reasonable rates. There are also plenty of places to grab snacks and drinks, while sporting and music events are regularly held in some of the public spaces.

Hili Fun City

Location Hili, Al Ain
Web hilifuncity.ae **Tel** 03 784 5542
Times Opening times vary
Price Dhs.45-50, free for kids up to
89cm tall
Map 3 p.213

This 22-hectare, spacious and leafy
park is the perfect out-of-town
setting for family outings. There is a
variety of arcade games and more
than 30 attractions, ranging from
gentle toddler rides, such as My First
Car, Safari and the Hili Express train,
to white-knuckle thrills for teens
and adults, like Thunderbolt and the
terrifying Sky Flyer. The park is being
gradually updated and there are more
rides on the way.

The park has an amphitheatre
where various singing, dancing and
circus shows are put on throughout
the day, should all the rides and
rollercoasters leave you in need of
something a little more sedate.

There are also plenty of grassy
spaces for picnics and BBQs; visitors
are welcome to arrive equipped with
their own well-stocked picnic baskets

Don't be fooled by Hili Fun
City's tame exterior. Nothing
prepares you for Sky Flyer,
a white-knuckle ride where
you hold on for dear life as
you swing like a pendulum
until you're upside down.

that the whole family can enjoy under
the shade of a tree while the little
ones play on the lawns. If you forget a
snack or two, don't worry as there are
refreshment stands too.

The park is open 16:00 to 22:00
(Monday to Thursday), 12:00 to
22:00 (Friday and Saturday), with
Wednesdays reserved for ladies and
children only. The park is closed on
Sundays and during Ramadan.

04

Abu Dhabi Falcon Hospital

Location Al Samkha **Web** falconhospital.com
Tel 02 575 5155 **Times** Tours at 10:00 and 14:00 (Sunday to Thursday)
Price Guide Dhs.170 (Adult), Dhs.80 (Child) **Map** 4 p.213

The falcon is one of the great symbols of Arabia, initially revered for its hunting skills. Today, falconry is one of the proudest and most prestigious traditional sports practised throughout the Gulf. The tour at the Abu Dhabi Falcon Hospital is a fascinating insight into falcons, their importance in local culture, the history of falconry and the role of the falcon today.

The two-hour tour is genuinely interactive, and visitors have the chance to get up close and personal to falcons and falcon handlers, as well as see these magnificent birds in action.

Abu Dhabi Falcon Hospital originally opened in 1999 as a purely veterinary facility but has gone on to become one of the leading centres of its kind in the world, with a team of specialists providing diagnosis, treatment and disease prevention for falcons, other bird species and even poultry.

Also found on the same site is the Abu Dhabi Animal Shelter but, if you're an animal lover, you may want to give that a swerve, as a cute Saluki in need of adoption may mean you leave Abu Dhabi with a bigger souvenir than you'd planned!

05

Ferrari World

Location Yas Island West **Web** ferrariworldabudhabi.com
Tel 02 496 8001 **Times** 11:00-20:00, closed on Mondays
Price Guide Dhs.195-385 **Map** **5** p.224

Part theme park, part simulator and part museum/learning centre for the legendary Italian brand, Ferrari World has won the hearts of UAE petrolheads and visitors alike. Out-and-out theme park fans should be impressed by the Formula Rossa – billed as the world's fastest rollercoaster, it reaches speeds of up to 240kmph. It's so fast riders have to wear safety goggles. The G-forces an F1 driver experiences are imitated by a 62-metre high ride that drops vertically through the park's roof, while a flume style water ride leads visitors through a series of twists, turns, rises and falls based on the workings of a Ferrari 599.

State-of-the-art simulators used to train Ferrari drivers give a realistic experience of being in the break-neck hustle and bustle of a real grand prix, while young wannabe Schumachers and Alonsos can attend a drivers' school. And anyone who has ever wanted, well, just about anything adorned with the famous 'prancing horse' logo, won't go home disappointed after a visit to the store.

If thrills and spills aren't your thing, then visit Bell'Italia for an aerial tour of a miniature Italy. Also, all manner of traditional Italian foods and flavours are on offer at dining outlets around the park. Fun for all the family, and all ages.

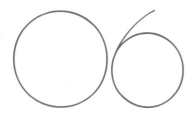

Al Ain Zoo

Location Sha'ab Al Ashkher, Al Ain **Web** alainzoo.ae **Tel** 03 799 2000
Times Various, open daily **Price Guide** Dhs.15 (Adults),
Dhs.5 (Three to 12), free (Under 3) **Map** 6 p.213

Stretching over 900 hectares, this is the largest and best zoo in the region. With ample greenery, a casual stroll through the paths that criss-cross the park makes for a wonderful family day out. As well as seeing apes, reptiles and big cats, you can get up close to local species such as the Arabian oryx and sand gazelle, or pay a visit to the fantastic birdhouse. The zoo is a centre for endangered species conservation and visitors can look forward to spotting true rarities. Nearly 30% of the 180 species are endangered and the park is even home to a stunning pair of white tigers and white lions. Family nights with fun activities take place on Wednesdays. A park train regularly departs from the central concourse, providing a whirlwind tour. Given its sprawling size, the easiest way to explore the zoo is to purchase the service of a buggy and driver when you buy your tickets. It's best to get there early to enjoy the cooler temperatures and quieter crowds.

Children and adults alike are sure to be delighted by a trip to the giraffe feeding station where, you can purchase a cup of carrots for Dhs.30 and use it to feed these fun, long-necked creatures by hand.

Yas Waterworld

Location Yas Island West **Web** yaswaterworld.com
Tel 02 414 2000 **Times** Opens at 10:00, closing time varies
Price Guide Dhs.185-385 **Map** **7** p.224

Yas Waterworld burst on to the scene at the end of 2012 achieving the seemingly impossible – in a country that boasts some of the best waterparks that can be found anywhere in the world, it managed to raise the bar even higher.

The large park is based on an ancient Arabian tale involving the search for a lost pearl, and it draws on this to combine touches of the traditional (the architecture and souk-style shopping and refreshment areas) with the very latest in water entertainment and technology. There are 43 rides, slides and attractions in total. As well as exciting kids' pools, a long lazy river and an interactive pearl diving attraction, the park has some incredible white-knuckle fun.

The Aqualoop spins riders 360 degrees around in a loop, while the Water Bomber rollercoaster is the region's first suspended coaster, reaching speeds of up to 55kmph; there's also a six-person tornado ride.

Wadi Adventure

Location Jebel Hafeet, Al Ain **Web** wadiadventure.ae
Tel 03 781 8422 **Times** 10:00-22:00 (Tuesday to Sunday), Surf Morning
07:00-10:00 (Friday to Saturday) **Price Guide** Dhs.100+ **Map** 8 p.213

Wadi Adventure is the first facility of its kind anywhere in the Middle East.

Perhaps the best way to think of Wadi Adventure is as a waterpark with a difference; instead of slides and rides, here you'll find three world-class white water rafting and kayaking runs, totalling more than a kilometre in length. Whether you choose to get stuck in with a rafting session or take a one-on-one kayak session, there are enough options to suit your needs and past experience. A giant conveyor belt drags you to the summit of the rapids and then it's up to you to complete the course. The beginner rapids are suitable for families (kids have to be taller than 1.2 metres). Don't be surprised if you capsize on the tougher rapids; just make sure you listen carefully to the safety instructions.

If water isn't your thing, then the tree-top obstacles and canyon swings should keep you occupied. There are also a few food and drink outlets for refuelling.

Surfer dudes can also get in on the action with a huge surf pool that generates a three-metre high wave every 90 seconds; while the more experienced surfers tackle the big waves at the back of the pool, beginners can take lessons nearer the shore.

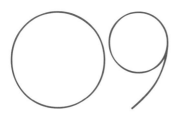

Zayed Sports City

Location Al Madina Al Riyadiya **Web** zsc.ae
Tel 02 403 4200 **Times** Varies **Price Guide** Varies
Map 9 p.218

Zayed Sports City is a sports and entertainment destination with plenty for the whole family to enjoy. Open seven days a week, it has an Olympic size and standard ice rink, where you can skate or even learn to figure skate or play ice hockey.

The complex also has a tennis centre, with lessons again available, and it is the first place in the UAE to offer the fun sport of padel tennis, which is booming in Spain and South America in particular. The Khalifa International Bowling Centre has a whopping 40 lanes of ten-pin bowling, as well as the usual array of food stands and video games.

There are even bumper cars for younger kids. The centrepiece of Zayed Sports City is the UAE's largest stadium, which plays host to major international events throughout the year, such as the UAE football finals.

English Premier League team Manchester City, which of course has strong links to Abu Dhabi, has a football school based at Zayed Sports City, where City's top coaches and players often take part in training sessions.

Al Forsan

Location Madinat Khalifa **Web** alforsan.com **Tel** 02 556 8555
Times 13:00-22:00 (Sunday to Thursday), 10:00-22:00 (Friday to Saturday)
Price Guide Dhs.55 with Dhs.25 credit **Map** **10** p.221

From the entrance, Al Forsan International Sports Resort looks no different to any other five-star resort but, as you walk through the grounds, you'll uncover its amazing assets.

Firstly, there are two large cable parks. One of the lakes at Al Forsan is dedicated to beginner boarders. Over on the expert lake, wakeboarders and wakeskaters zip their way around the outside of the lake, jumping over ramps while practising surface switches and superhuman tricks.

Al Forsan also offers some incredible paintballing fields, as well as clay pigeon shooting, archery and horse riding. The motorsports centre offers up a range of petrol-powered activities. There's a 1.2km CIK-approved circuit and vehicles with top speeds of up to 120kmph available (for experienced karters); there's also a kids' karting track. The dual circuit, fully-floodlit, off-road buggy track allows two buggies to race without any chance of collision.

If you've ever dreamed of becoming a daredevil stunt driver, there's an alternative circuit at Al Forsan where you can learn the arts of drifting, skid controls and power turns.

نـادي أبـوظبـي الـريـاضـي
Abu Dhabi Country Club

Mondo Pizzeria

The home of contemporary & traditional Italian cuisine

Sardinia
Fine Dining

A culinary cruise along the shores of the Mediterranean

19 Al Saada Street, Al Mushrif Abu Dhabi, UAE P.O. Box 47776
Tel: +971 2 657 7777 Fax: +971 2 445 4112 Web: www.adcountryclub.com

Showstopper Restaurants

Fishmarket 50

Pachaylen 51

Quest 52

Tiara 54

Mawal 56

Le Deck 57

Marco Pierre White Steakhouse and Grill 58

Ushna 60

Chamas Churrascaria and Bar 61

Mezlai 63

Fairmont Bab Al Bahr

Showstopper
Restaurants
Introduction

Abu Dhabi's gastronomic landscape is a tasty battleground with celebrity chefs competing against bargain ethnic eateries to win your hard-earned cash.

Variety is the spice of life where Abu Dhabi's restaurant scene is concerned, with all the nationalities that now call this city home bringing their own particular specialities and flavours to bear on local gastronomy. You will truly find everything from molecular gastronomy to Mexican-inspired pub grub and back-street curry houses, and they're all equally delicious.

Many of Abu Dhabi's most beloved restaurants are located within hotels and leisure clubs, and their popularity is partly down to the fact that these are virtually the only outlets where you can drink alcohol with your meal. Almost all other restaurants are unlicensed. If you're the type who requires a glass of vino to make a meal complete, it's best to phone ahead to check whether the establishment serves alcohol. There's quite a hefty mark-up on drinks, with a decent bottle of wine often costing as much as your meal. But the city has some superb independent restaurants and cafes that shouldn't be ignored just because they don't serve booze. Some are ethnic eateries lining the streets of Abu Dhabi's oldest areas, while others are fresh food cafes and juice bars located in the big malls.

However, as much as there are cheap eats and reasonable offers, Abu Dhabi is best known for its over-the-top lavishness and this applies to its restaurants as much as everything else. Big name celebrity chefs rub shoulders with Michelin-starred culinary giants in Abu Dhabi; Marco Pierre White helms a couple of restaurants at the Fairmont Bab Al Bahr (p.113), celeb Emirati chef Ali Salem Edbowa is head chef at Emirates Palace's Mezlai (p.63), and Gary Rhodes is set to open Rhodes 44 at the St Regis (p.10) in 2013. There are also hospitality uber-brands like Hakkasan in the mix.

These names alone speak volumes about the sheer variety of high-end food on offer in the city, while plenty of other top-class eateries that may not (yet!) boast a famous chef or a globally-recognised name are forging their own reputations through quality and creativity.

Ramadan Dining

During Ramadan, opening and closing times of restaurants change considerably. Because eating and drinking in public is forbidden during daylight hours, many places only open after sunset then keep going well into the early hours. The breaking of the fast (iftar) is popular with both fasting Muslims and non-fasting expats keen to try the traditional local delicacies. The practice of suhoor (think of it as the midnight feast that sustains Muslims through the following day's fast) has also become a more communal event that people of all religious backgrounds take part in during Ramadan.

Fishmarket

Location InterContinental Abu Dhabi
Web dining-intercontinental-ad.ae **Tel** 02 666 6888
Times 12:30-16:00 and 19:00-23:00 **Map** 1 p.214

If you're a seafood fan, then the chances are that Fishmarket will quickly be added to your list of favourites once you've scoffed down some of the catches of the day that are served up at this marina-side venue.

The concept is simplicity itself. Guests are confronted by an extensive array of fresh seafood, along with a cartload of fresh vegetables, and a range of noodle and rice varieties. Take a look, see what tickles your fancy, and then opt for a fish, the style of cooking (grilled, sautéed or fried) and let the chef know what kind of sauce (green curry, red curry or oyster sauce) and accompaniments most float your boat.

Portions tend to err on the side of gargantuan, but the flavours are sensational and the fish is as fresh as it gets. The shack-style, tropical island decor and the always smiley service, make Fishmarket feel a long way from Abu Dhabi, and it's an easy place to relax and have fun. A word of warning: the menu concentrates almost solely on seafood with few choices for carnivores and vegetarians.

The rope-bound bamboo pillars, sailor-blue tablecloths and lobster-filled fish tanks give Fishmarket a rustic seaside shack feel – the perfect setting to enjoy fresh grilled red snapper, jumbo prawns or local hammour.

Pachaylen

Location Eastern Mangroves Hotel & Spa by Anantara
Web anantara.com **Tel** 02 656 1000 **Times** 12:30-15:30 and 18:30-23:00
Map 2 p.217

If the rest of Eastern Mangroves is a delicate balance between the Arabian and the Far Eastern, then its signature restaurant, Pachaylen, is a full-on embrace of Anantara's Thai heritage. From the all-Thai kitchen and waiting-on staff to the menu and the aromas pouring out from the open kitchen, it's authentic but sophisticated South East Asian through and through.

You'll be hard-pressed to find a more beautifully decked-out restaurant in Abu Dhabi and, if you're going to be picking up the tab, make sure you sit at the golden chair – there's one at each table and it's your right as the host!

You'll be equally hard-pressed to uncover a tastier, lovelier welcome than the traditional miang kham street snack that's served up as an amuse-bouche. After that, it's traditional Thai done in the tastiest way you'll find anywhere outside of Bangkok. The soft shell crab salad is the standout starter, while you should look no further than the slow-cooked Thai curries for your main course. It is all a long way from traditional street food, and the spiciness isn't overdone.

Pachaylen delivers again on dessert; the banana pancake spring rolls or sticky rice and fruit are the perfect ways to finish.

Quest

Location Jumeirah at Etihad Towers
Web jumeirah.com **Tel** 02 811 5666 **Times** 12:00-15.30 (Sunday to Thursday) and 19:00-23:30 (Sunday to Friday) **Map** **3** p.214

Abu Dhabi is jam-packed with very good restaurants but, until recently, it has lacked something really world-class when it comes to pioneering food and flavours. That's a gap that Quest fills with ease and a good splash of panache.

The restaurant is beautiful and elegant – all of the tables, spread around the equally dramatic open kitchen, offer incredible views from the 63rd floor. But, as Abu Dhabi sparkles below, it's the service – just about perfect – and the food that capture the attention. Officially, it's Pan-Asian fare, blending diverse flavours from Japan, Malaysia and China. However, this is the kind of Far Eastern cuisine that Heston Blumenthal or Ferran Adria might serve up: deconstructed and reinterpreted, never pretentious but intriguing, fun and downright tasty.

Salads are presented in plant pots, foie gras comes served on spoons, soup is created at the table, and popping candy 'pops up' in the desserts. For the full experience, try the tasting menu along with an accompanying selection of wines chosen by the sommelier (although it's fun to play with the iPad wine menu too). An exciting and truly innovative culinary experience.

Tiara

Location Burj Al Marina,
Marina Mall
Tel 02 681 9090
Times Open daily, noon-midnight
Map 4 p.214

After a short walk through the mall, and then an uplifting elevator ride to the 55th floor, you arrive at Tiara: Abu Dhabi's must-see revolving restaurant. The panoramic views from here are spectacular and worth the trip alone – but what better way to enjoy the capital's skyline and coastline than from the comfort of a dining chair with a hearty meal. It's easy to relax at the booth-style tables and in armchairs as you slowly watch the world go by – literally.

Adding to the unforgettable experience is an international menu, the highlight of which is the light and crispy calamari dunked in creamy aioli followed by a sumptuous seafood platter served with paella rice and sweetcorn and lime emulsion.

Lighter lunches and starters include crisp, crunchy Caesar salad with chicken or shrimp; smoked salmon tabbouleh; or a traditional seafood soup that's loaded with scallops and tiger shrimp. For larger appetites, the hearty portions of spicy penne arrabiata or creamy spinach tortellini are big on flavour too.

It's tasty fare served at a great height and, for a meal with a view, this is up there with the best.

> Don't forget the camera for ever-changing views of the city, then refuel on warm banana crumble or almond cake with blueberry sauce.

A TRULY ROYAL
DINING EXPERIENCE

High above the shoreline of Abu Dhabi, in the heart of its landmark Burj Al Marina Tower, sits the region's first ever five-stars, stand-alone revolving restaurant. Offering the only full panoramic view of the nation's capital, Tiara welcomes you to this unique dining experience. With a fusion of Mediterranean and Western cuisines, Tiara's menu has been designed and perfected by internationally renowned head chefs.

Indulge in the mouth watering menu whilst enjoying unbridled views of the Arabian Gulf, Emirates Palace and Abu Dhabi's beautiful Corniche. With one revolution every hour, you are guaranteed the best seats in the house, no matter where you sit.

Our meticulous silver service training ensures that your dining experience is truly a royal one.

Tiara Restaurant LLC
TRI – Burj Al Marina, Marina Mall, Abu Dhabi
P. O. Box 45954. Tel: 02 681 9090, Fax: 02 681 9441
Email: tiararestaurant@silsilaholding.com

05

Mawal

Location Hilton Abu Dhabi **Web** hilton.com **Tel** 02 681 1900
Times 12:30-00:30 (Saturday to Wednesday),
12:30-01:30 (Thursday and Friday) **Map** **5** p.214

Mawal is as much an experience as it is a restaurant and, especially if you're in the Middle East for the first time, a visit to this Lebanese eatery provides a real insight into the more traditional elements of regional food and entertainment.

Arabian belly dancing and singing top the bill at Mawal – and are perhaps the reasons that, in a city with plenty of Lebanese restaurants, Mawal is continually the most popular and lively. However, the excellent food and colourful service are enough to draw in the crowds in their own right.

In addition to an exhaustive range of hot and cold Lebanese mezze, there is a selection of kebabs grilled to perfection. If you plan to stay for the show, reservations are essential as the place comes alive later on. It starts at 22:30 Saturday to Wednesday and at 23:30 on Thursday and Friday, and the minimum spend on food is Dhs. 275 (weekdays) or Dhs. 325 (weekends) per person for the show.

Start your evening at The Jazz Bar, open Sunday to Friday at the Hilton Abu Dhabi. Sit back and relax with an expertly mixed cocktail and enjoy dazzling live music from the six-piece jazz band.

Le Deck

Location Monte-Carlo Beach Club **Web** montecarlobeachclub.ae
Tel 02 656 3500 **Times** 11:00-15:00 (Saturday to Thursday), 18:00-22:00
(Saturday to Wednesday), 18:00-23:00 (Thursday to Friday) **Map** 6 p.227

Located in the beautiful surroundings of Monte-Carlo Beach Club, with a terraced area that reaches towards the giant pool, Le Deck is a genuinely top class offering. The restaurant has an airily elegant feel to it, with the large open kitchen serving as the centrepiece. If the weather is agreeable – and it usually is – then pick a table out on the terrace.

The menu reflects the fresh, airy ambience of both the beach club and the restaurant; even heartier fare such as pumpkin and amaretto tortellini, risotto and the large assortment of steaks are treated with a lightness of touch, while the plentiful use of salads and fresh seasonings leave you feeling healthy and full.

The delicate flavours in dishes like the hazelnut and porcini veloute, the penne crab, or the half boneless chicken with sweet corn puree and popcorn, suggest confident and creative hands at work in the open kitchen. The day pass, spa treatment and lunch package offers excellent value for money. If you're only there for the food, then the degustation menu is a six-course journey into bliss.

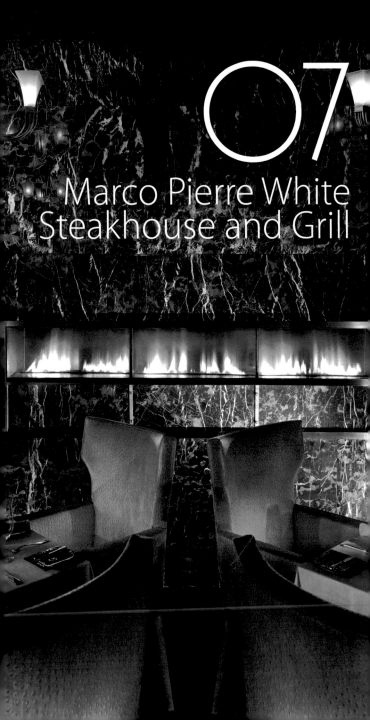

07
Marco Pierre White
Steakhouse and Grill

Does a beautifully appointed restaurant with exact yet friendly service, delivering British comfort food elevated to superb standards, sound like your idea of heaven? Then get to Marco Pierre White Steakhouse and Grill immediately.

A single bite of the foie gras starter tells you that Marco has brought all his experience to bear in his Abu Dhabi restaurant. And, while the flame-lit venue may look beautiful, it is anything but style over substance.

The menu is enough to give vegetarians nightmares – great cuts of meat take top billing here, alongside the superb wine list – but, even amongst some pretty stiff competition, it's the steaks that stand out. Tuck into a pepper sauce-topped fillet and you'll know why. The sumptuous surroundings will have you spending the whole night wallowing in this fine-dining, wine-fuelled experience.

The set menu with wine pairings is nothing short of exquisite: Scottish smoked salmon with slow poached quail egg; crab veloute with Alaskan king crab tortie; slow roasted Wagyu tenderloin; and Eton mess to finish – perfection on a plate.

Top 10 Family Venues

Dine Map **11** p.218
Aloft Abu Dhabi – 02 654 5121
Mondo Map **12** p.216
Abu Dhabi Country Club – 02 657 7785
Noodle House Map **13** p.219
Souk at Qaryat Al Beri – 02 558 1699
Choices Brunch Map **14** p.224
Yas Island Rotana – 02 656 4000
CuiScene Map **15** p.219
Fairmont Bab Al Bahr – 02 654 3238
La Mamma Map **16** p.216
Sheraton Abu Dhabi – 02 697 0224
Jones The Grocer Map **17** p.216
Al Muroor – 02 443 8762
Zest Map **18** p.213
Al Ain Rotana – 03 754 5111
Shakespeare & Co. Map **19** p.215
Central Market – 02 639 9626
Stars 'n' Bars Map **20** p.224
Yas Marina & Yacht Club – 02 565 0101

If you fancy a more casual affair, pop next door to Frankie's, a bustling Italian managed by jockey Frankie Dettori and MPW himself.

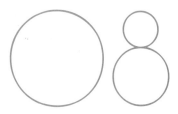

Ushna

Location The Souk at Qaryat Al Beri **Tel** 02 558 1769
Times 12:30-23:30 (Weekdays), 12:30-00:30 (Weekends)
Map 8 p.219

Another of the venues that is making the Souk at Qaryat Al Beri the gastronomic epicentre of Abu Dhabi, Ushna is an Indian restaurant – but not as you know it. It is Indian cuisine filtered through a prism of high-end dining, and Ushna's sophisticated surroundings perfectly complement the beautifully prepared food.

Punjabi classics like lamb pasanda, aloo tikki ragda, tandoori murgh and paneer are all delicately flavoured and never over-spiced, allowing the quality of the produce to shine. The curries are, of course, sensational, and side orders like aloo jeera, dal and rice are just as good. If you have room, the freshly-prepared breads are almost meals in their own right and well worth sharing.

The service mirrors the superb setting and there's a good selection of premium wines and cocktails to choose from. During the cooler months, bag a table by the water overlooking the Grand Mosque for a romantic night out.

> Vegetarian dishes include tandoori sabzi – glazed mixed vegetables marinated in vinegar and spices and cooked in a clay oven; or gobhi ke sabzi – an excellent Indian homemade delicacy of fresh cauliflower with ginger and tomatoes, to name but a few.

Chamas
Churrascaria and Bar

Location InterContinental Abu Dhabi
Web dining-intercontinental-ad.ae **Tel** 02 6666 6888
Times 18:00-23:30 (Daily), 12:00-16:00 (Friday)
Map 9 p.214

Vegetarian treats, molecular gastronomic wonders, haute cuisine creations, fresh seafood snacks… these all have their place in the culinary landscape, of course, but when it comes to pure, gluttonous, over-eating joy, surely nothing comes close to the caveman appeal of meat, meat and more meat.

If that sounds like your idea of perfection, then Chamas is the Brazilian restaurant where dreams come true. Eat as much red meat as you like for a fixed price; Chamas' concept is great but the road to carnivorous bliss is a long one. First, you need to navigate (but mostly skip past) the salad bar, before steering through steaming bowls of polenta, hash browns, black beans, vegetable rice and fried bananas. Resist all of these wayside temptations and you'll finally arrive at various barbecued

meats and steak heaven, with sirloin, flank, rib eye and tenderloin all being served up.

The restaurant is suitably noisy and frantic, with an entertaining band knocking out samba, making it great for large groups. It is generally packed every night, proving that Chamas has got the formula for Brazilian churrascaria just right.

Mezlai

Location Emirates Palace **Web** kempinski.com
Tel 02 690 7999 **Times** 13:00-22:30 (Monday to Sunday)
Map 10 p.214

Mezlai is a fairly unique offering. For starters, it has a celebrity head chef that very few guests will have heard of – Ali Salem Edbowa is a regular on local TV stations and is one of a handful of skilful kitchen maestros who are helping to raise the art and profile of Gulf cuisine.

Mezlai means 'the old lock of the door', which aptly reflects its ability to unlock the secrets of authentic Emirati cuisine to both a local and international audience. As befits an establishment that prides itself on being the UAE's first Emirati restaurant, Mezlai's Arabic-themed decor features plenty of intricate and well thought out design touches, such as majlis corners and memorabilia from the country's early days. The stained glass lanterns may be traditional but they also serve to cast an atmospheric spell over proceedings.

In terms of ingredients, you'll find few surprises; the food relies on traditional staples like rice, meat and fish. But dishes are prepared with a sprinkling of regional influences from across the Middle East. True to the UAE's culinary traditions, there's an emphasis on seafood and you'll sample specialities like Weld-Al Walad – shark soup – and grilled Gulf hammour, while carnivores are treated to camel meat and lamb medfoun.

> Mezlai is not the only culinary gem at the Emirates Palace. Be sure to explore the dining delights at chic seafood brasserie Sayad (the Arabic word for 'fisherman') and the award-winning, authentic Italian eatery Mezzaluna.

© Emirates Palace

Best Bars

Skylite 68

Sho Cho 69

The Beachcomber 70

Impressions 71

Lemon & Lime 74

Left Bank 75

Pearls & Caviar 76

Cloud Nine – Cigar and Champagne Bar 78

Allure by Cipriani 79

Relax@12 81

Best Bars
Introduction

The days when Abu Dhabi's bar scene was little more than a sandy backwater of British pub is long gone; and what you'll find today is an eclectic and exciting nightlife.

Standards are high in Abu Dhabi, due to the particular demands of the city's utterly unique and multicultural drinking crowd. The city's community is such an eclectic mix of creeds and kinds that there's an incredibly varied range of drink and bar expectations. So, have these expectations been met? Indeed, they have – Abu Dhabi has responded to the challenge by 'raising the bars' to create a parade of interesting and atmospheric venues vying to meet every drinker's desire.

From the downright dirty (but fun) dive bars of downtown to some of the world's most glamorous and renowned celebrity party venues, Abu Dhabi has it all, with every bar attempting to stand out among the city's five-star fleet. Maybe you're in a boardies and flip-flops mood and after a laidback sundowner? Or perhaps you're looking to throw on your swankiest threads and take to the town for a raucous night that you'll never remember? The city bows to your every request.

Although, due to the taxes levied on alcohol, drinking in Abu Dhabi can be fairly costly, the city is also bulging with inventive promotions and theme nights that allow you to get merry without paying over the odds. The fairer sex, in particular, can paint the town red without spending a fil thanks to the whole host of drink-specific ladies nights that take place during the week – usually on Monday, Tuesday or Wednesday.

When it comes to bar itineraries, Abu Dhabi can offer a more varied night out than many other cities, since punters are able to hop into a taxi and zoom between bar stools at opposite sides of the city quickly and cheaply.

The venues listed in this chapter highlight the various types of bars in Abu Dhabi, both in terms of style and location. Obviously, personal preference plays a significant part in such a list, so keep in mind that these were chosen to emphasise the different varieties in the city; there's not just one bar with great views, one place for sundowners or one beach bar to hit for laid-back cocktails – these are just some of the best and most popular haunts.

So, whether you're looking for that quirky one-of-a-kind bar, a suave cigar lounge or a sticky floored dingy dive club, Abu Dhabi has it all. And, if it doesn't exist right now, it probably will next week!

Door Policy

Certain bars and nightclubs have a selective entry policy. Sometimes 'membership' is introduced to control the clientele, but it is often only enforced during busy periods or to disallow entry for certain groups. Large groups (especially those consisting of all males) and singles, for example, may be turned away from busier bars and clubs without much of an explanation. Avoid the inconvenience by breaking the group up or by going in a mixed-gender group. Some of the city's most popular hotspots can be nearly impossible to enter on certain nights unless you're on the guest list, so be sure to call and book in advance.

Skylite

Location Yas Viceroy
Web viceroyhotelsandresorts.com
Tel 02 656 0600 **Times** 19:00-
01:00 (Sunday to Wednesday),
19:00-02:00 (Thursday and Friday)
Map 1 p.224

Another bar at Yas Viceroy, Rush, is also worth visiting as it is located in the bridge that straddles the race track, with interiors and a cocktail list that live up to this stunning setting.

When you head out in Abu Dhabi for the first time, you want to go somewhere super-stylish that makes a statement, and venues don't come much swankier than Skylite. Perched on the roof of the iconic Yas Viceroy hotel, the stunning views from this rooftop lounge bar will blow you away, and even the most style conscious will appreciate the modern, imaginative decor. After

all, if it's a good enough bar for the Hollywood A-listers that attend the annual F1 GP to come to party…

There are light bites and long wine, champagne and cocktail lists to choose from, while the dress code errs on the smarter and trendier side of casual. The best time to enjoy Skylite is as the sun goes down, but it's easy enough to spend all night here too.

02

Sho Cho

Location The Souk at Qaryat Al Beri **Web** sho-cho.com
Tel 02 558 1117 **Times** 12:00-14:45 and 18:00-23:45 (Sunday to
Thursday), 12:00-23:45 (Friday and Saturday)
Map 2 p.219

For a while now, Sho Cho's fun brand of sushi and cocktails teamed with modern Japanese style had made it one of Dubai's most achingly hip restaurants and nightspots, so the residents of Abu Dhabi were overjoyed to find that Sho Cho had successfully made the leap to the capital. All the same elements have been retained – the interiors are a real delight, while the decking area boasts the incredible creekside views that are almost par for the course at Qaryat Al Beri.

The cuisine is perhaps best described as oriental fusion, with plenty of fish and sushi dishes on the menu, including maki rolls, tempura, sashimi, salads and appetisers such as soft shell crab spring roll and king fish ceviche. The brunches (Friday lunchtime and Sunday evening) are extremely popular, but describing Sho Cho as a restaurant is misleading given that it has fast become a favourite among Abu Dhabi's party-loving socialites.

Guest DJs and live bands are regularly brought in to provide the soundtracks, with Wednesday's ladies' night (two free vodka martinis) one of the most popular in the city.

03

The Beachcomber

Location Sheraton Abu Dhabi Hotel & Resort
Web sheratonabudhabihotel.com
Tel 02 677 3333 **Times** 16:00-01:00 (Daily)
Map 3 p.216

With Abu Dhabi's reputation for A-list venues, you'd be forgiven for thinking that all its bars are simply places for the beautiful people to be seen. But there are plenty of alternatives on offer too and, if your idea of a good bar is a little more relaxed, then head for The Beachcomber.

Sat between the pool and the private lagoon at Sheraton Abu Dhabi, this chilled-out beach bar feels more Caribbean than Arabian, which makes it popular with after-work and weekend crowds, as well as holidaymakers. It serves up a tapas menu that, while not authentically Spanish, does provide the ideal accompaniment to the cocktails that are on offer.

Impressions

Location Eastern Mangroves Hotel & Spa by Anantara
Web anantara.com **Tel** 02 656 1000
Times 18:00-21:00, lounge open until 01:00
Map 4 p.217

Fantastic views are almost taken for granted amongst Abu Dhabi's top bars and clubs. You want beach views, a dramatic cityscape, maybe an island panorama? No problem at all. While these views may still be sensational, after enjoying the sights from one or two venues, you can begin to think that you'll never be dumbfounded by another sensational skyline again… until you arrive at Impressions which, suitably, makes quite the impression. Located on the top floor of Eastern Mangroves, stare out from the terrace or through the huge glass doors here, and you're faced with nothing but islands and endless mangroves – in spite of the fact that the city centre is just minutes away.

The bar itself is all totally top draw – from the sumptuous decor to the equally extravagant wine list – but,

be warned, the prices match the high standards. The atmosphere is perhaps a little more formal than some other champagne bars, but this makes for a nice change. Champagne, cocktails and good scotch are what this bar was made for, and the snacks take the form of cheese platters rather than the usual tapas.

Sip on perfectly mixed cocktails as the sun sets over a luxurious oasis in the midst of the mystic Liwa Desert.

Suhail at Qasr al Sarab Desert Resort by Anantara

Lemon & Lime

Location The Westin Abu Dhabi Golf Resort & Spa, Sas Al Nakhl Island
Web westinabudhabigolfresort.com **Tel** 02 616 9999
Times 17:00-01:00 (Daily) **Map** 5 p.220

Lemon & Lime is a venue tailor-made for epicureans who prefer their nights to be focused on quality rather than decibels. This extremely elegant wine and cigar bar is the kind of place where you can get together to start your night, or simply spend the whole evening soaking up the chic atmosphere. Its off-island location means it is usually busy rather than jam-packed, which perfectly suits the laid-back sophistication of the venue.

The decor is contemporary luxury, although the amazing golf course views dominate. There's an excellent pianist who tinkles the ivories seductively earlier in the evening, and ramps it up a little as the night gets going.

The variety of wines on offer is exceptional. Fans of fine vintages should keep their eye out for the regular wine and champagne offers, and the one-off special events, which provide real value for money.

Left Bank

Location The Souk at Qaryat Al Beri **Web** emiratesleisureretail.com
Tel 02 558 1680 **Times** 17:00 until close (Saturday to Thursday),
12:30 until close (Friday) **Map** 6 p.219

Against the exaggerated opulence of Abu Dhabi's bar scene, Left Bank comes across as something relatively simple, even though this lovely bar would turn heads in almost any city in the world. The appeal perhaps lies in that international and metropolitan feel – Left Bank would be just as well-suited to Madrid, New York or, indeed, Paris as it is to its beautiful location in the Souk at Qaryat Al Beri.

However, with views of Sheikh Zayed Grand Mosque and a terrace that has touches of Arabian influence, there's no mistaking that you're in Abu Dhabi. The cuisine on offer is contemporary European fusion, while the interior echoes a variety of exclusive London venues, complete with a VIP section and inexhaustible cocktail menu. Visitors are advised to book ahead if they want a table.

Tuck into mains such as mini fishcakes with truffled hollandaise, mini burgers, or mini chicken and beef souvlakis with tzatziki – the perfect accompaniment to a passion fruit mojito. Or order a pitcher of sangria with a welcome sharing platter. Yum!

07

Pearls & Caviar

Location Shangri-La Hotel, Qaryat Al Beri
Web pearlsandcaviar.com **Tel** 02 509 8777
Times 19:00-23:30 (Sunday to Thursday),
20:00-23:30 (Friday) **Map** 7 p.219

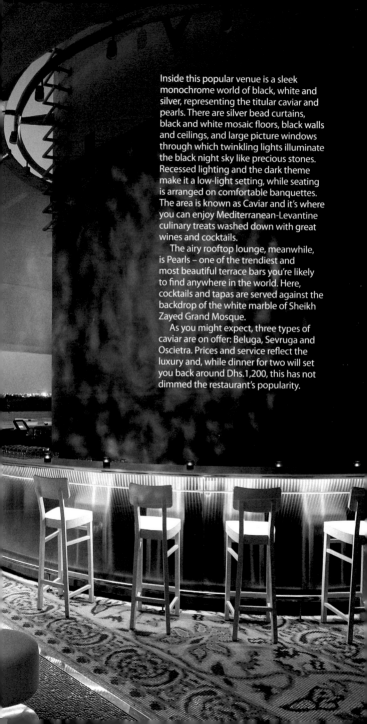

Inside this popular venue is a sleek monochrome world of black, white and silver, representing the titular caviar and pearls. There are silver bead curtains, black and white mosaic floors, black walls and ceilings, and large picture windows through which twinkling lights illuminate the black night sky like precious stones. Recessed lighting and the dark theme make it a low-light setting, while seating is arranged on comfortable banquettes. The area is known as Caviar and it's where you can enjoy Mediterranean-Levantine culinary treats washed down with great wines and cocktails.

The airy rooftop lounge, meanwhile, is Pearls – one of the trendiest and most beautiful terrace bars you're likely to find anywhere in the world. Here, cocktails and tapas are served against the backdrop of the white marble of Sheikh Zayed Grand Mosque.

As you might expect, three types of caviar are on offer: Beluga, Sevruga and Oscietra. Prices and service reflect the luxury and, while dinner for two will set you back around Dhs.1,200, this has not dimmed the restaurant's popularity.

Cloud Nine – Cigar and Champagne Bar

Location Sheraton Abu Dhabi Hotel & Resort
Web sheratonabudhabihotel.com **Tel** 02 677 3333
Times 17:00-02:00 (Daily) **Map** 8 p.216

Cloud Nine understands that not every night out is about dancing and sickly sweet cocktails; it's a bar that whispers softly to ladies and gentlemen of a more sophisticated palate and select sensibility. If a refined evening of cognac, caviar and the finest cigars appeals to you, then this is a place you'll want to call home.

From the first cut of your hand-picked Cohiba, Monte Cristo or Bolivar (delivered to you on a silver platter, of course), to the last delicious mouthful of Beluga that passes your lips, this luxurious venue exudes a pleasing mix of

old boys' club charm and trendy sophistication. If caviar doesn't do it for you, then plenty of other delicate snacks are available to accompany your whisky or glass of bubbly.

Service is pleasant and discreet, and a pianist adds further elegance to a classy evening out.

The 'Sheraton Social Hour' takes place between 19:00 and 20:00 on Monday, Wednesday and Saturday and is a delightful offer; the hotel wine expert serves up (and talks about) a variety of special, assorted wines that cost just Dhs.25 a glass during the offer and change each time.

Allure by Cipriani

Location Yas Yacht Club **Web** nightcluballure.com
Tel 02 657 5400 **Times** Thursday and Friday nights
Map 9 p.224

Located in the Yas Yacht Club, Allure by Cipriani is a night spot that manages to achieve sophistication without pretension, and is popular with music-loving revellers who want a bar where they can dance the night away. It's still definitely high-end – there is, after all, a Dhs.68,000 bottle of champagne on the menu – but Allure strives to provide more of a European or Ibiza dance bar groove than the typical posh club.

The all-white decor is stunning, with LED lights spanning the length of the tessellated ceiling. The screen above the DJ booth, where top international DJs regularly conduct proceedings, provides stunning visuals. Benches and tables are grouped in the centre of the dance area, which is surrounded by VIP pods.

It's mainly a drinking and dancing venue, but, should hunger strike, you can order sushi snacks from sister restaurant Yotto. There are also regular theme nights and club nights that feature dancers, European DJs and impressive visual effects.

Relax@12

Location Aloft Abu Dhabi **Web** relaxat12.com
Tel 02 654 5183 **Times** 17:00 until 02:00 (Weekdays)
and 03:00 (Weekends)
Map 10 p.218

If rooftop cocktails, heady views and a spot of sushi sound like your idea of bliss – and, let's face it, why wouldn't they? – then you're going to love spending time at Relax@12.

This isn't some high-octane nightspot; the name says it all – chill out in the sleek lounge, nibble on some Asian bites and down a cocktail or two as you sink into one of the inviting sofas on the terrace overlooking Abu Dhabi's gorgeous skyline from a quieter spot at the foot of the island. The decor is retro-modern, with glowing bars, dim lighting and angular furniture throughout, and both the terrace and huge-windowed bar attract a refreshingly broad mix of clientele.

The striking view alone is worth a visit, but the extensive menu of beer, wine and cocktails, along with delicious sushi and Japanese snacks, makes this a perfect spot for both visitors and locals.

Relax@12 is also a venue that works hard to provide value to guests, with offers on throughout the week or year, weekly ladies' nights, and regular Club So-Hi nights.

Party on the rooftop at Club So-Hi by Relax@12 with pop-rock favourites on Tuesdays, your guilty pleasure of 80s, 90s and 00s on Wednesdays, and a global fusion of rock and r'n'b on Thursdays.

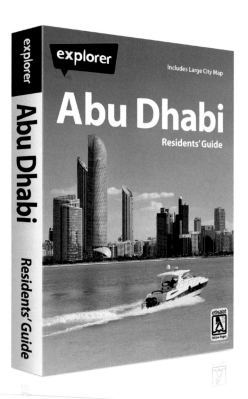

Shopping
Spots

Abu Dhabi Mall 87

Souk Al Bawadi 88

The Gold Souk 89

Dalma Mall 90

Khalidiyah Mall 91

Central Market 93

Fish, Fruit & Vegetable Souk 94

Iranian Souk 95

BAS Mall 96

Marina Mall 97

Shopping

Abu Dhabi Mall

Shopping
Spots
Introduction

With souks, boutiques and mammoth malls at every turn, you won't have any problems spending your hard-earned cash while out and about in Abu Dhabi.

Abu Dhabi provides many opportunities to indulge in a shopping spree; with countless malls, souks and markets to choose from, the desert city is a true shopaholic's dream where you can buy just about anything and everything.

Mega-malls such as Marina Mall (p.97) and Abu Dhabi Mall (p.87) are famed as gleaming hubs of trade filled with a mix of international high street brands and plush designer names. Practicality plays a large part in the local mall culture and, during the hotter months, these malls are oases of cool in the sweltering city - somewhere to walk, shop, eat and be entertained away from the soaring heat outside.

But shopping in Abu Dhabi is not purely about mall-trawling. Indeed, some of the city's best shopping spots are to be found outside the malls – venture a bit further and you can find yourself in an atmospheric souk shopping for gold (p.89). The souks, Arabia's traditional market places, provide a slightly more original way to shop; bargaining is very much a part of the experience and, instead of branded shops, you'll find small independent shopkeepers and stalls marketing their wares in an atmospheric setting.

In addition to specialist souks, there are a number of places where a broad range of items, including souvenirs and traditional gifts, are sold. Shopping spots around Electra Street and Hamdan Bin Mohammed Street are examples of places where you can shop to your heart's content in a non-mall setting.

Bargaining is still common practice in the souks and other traditional shopping areas of the UAE; you'll need to give it a go to get the best prices. Before you take the plunge, try to get an idea of prices from a few shops, as there can often be a significant difference. Once you've decided how much you are willing to spend, offer an initial bid that is roughly around half that price. Stay laidback and vaguely disinterested in general. When your initial offer is rejected (and it will be), keep going until you reach an agreement or until you have reached your own limit. If the price isn't right, say so and walk out – the vendor will often follow and suggest a compromise price. As a general rule, the more you buy, the better the discount. When the price is agreed, it is considered bad form to back out of the sale.

Shopping Hours
The UAE is the world capital of shopping and, with most shops open seven days a week, you'll have no trouble tracking down the goods you desire. With most malls open from around 09:00 until at least 22:00 every night, and some until midnight at the weekends, there's plenty of time to browse.

Abu Dhabi Mall

Location Tourist Club Area **Web** abudhabi-mall.com
Tel 02 645 4858 **Times** 10:00-22:00 (Sunday to Wednesday),
10:00-23:00 (Thursday), 15:30-11:00 (Friday)
Map **1** p.216

This is arguably the main destination for shopaholics visiting Abu Dhabi, with more than 200 retail outlets spread over four floors. It has a broad range of shops and is particularly good if you're looking for jewellery or gifts. The shops that really bring in the shoppers are the Paris Gallery and Virgin Megastore which, as well as music, games and DVDs, also sells tickets to local events.

> Abu Dhabi Mall hosts exciting seasonal events throughout the year, including the popular Winter Fest in December. A Christmas market takes over the walkways of the mall, and there's Santa's Wonderland for the kids.

There are some gems in terms of smaller boutiques, such as The White Company, while there are plenty of jewellers offering signature pieces at excellent prices and a few shops selling local paraphernalia. Visiting Abu Dhabi Mall is about more than just shopping, however, and there are restaurants on every floor, as well as a nine-screen Cineplex, a food court and a children's play area. The 3,000 covered parking spaces and the taxi rank mean you won't struggle to get back to your hotel.

Abu Dhabi Mall is particularly good at looking after the needs of visiting families; baby trolleys are available for hire, and you can pick them up next to Mugg & Bean on level one. The cafe is a good place to stop for a pre-shop breakfast. The mall also rents electric wheelchairs at the customer service desk on level one.

Souk Al Bawadi

Location Bawadi Mall, Al Ain
Web bawadimall.com
Map 2 p.213

If you make the journey to Abu Dhabi's second city, Al Ain (p.202), this souk and market is a must-see attraction. The modern complex was purpose-built to accommodate the move of the old livestock market from the town centre a few years ago. While the livestock is no longer sold from the back of broken-down pick-ups balancing on stilts, the charm of the old souk has been maintained in this new environment. As is often the case, it's the characters of the people that create the atmosphere – and that remains the same.

The animal pens are neatly lined up under shaded protection and generally sectioned by type and breed. There's a great variety of typical Emirati farming animals on display, from new-born goats and camels to enormous dairy cows and shorn sheep. You won't get crowds of tourists here – this really is an authentic local trading experience and a wonderful insight into the rural business of purchasing and trading livestock and agricultural goods.

As well as the livestock, the souk area offers over 50 stalls of traditional and agricultural items such as fertilisers, firewood, nursery plants, pet supplies and fencing, as well as vet services and small cafes.

Revisit the past at Bawadi Mall's Heritage Village – an indoor-outdoor souk selling merchandise such as gold, handicrafts, carpets, pottery and more. Or, stay in the present and visit the mall's entertainment centre with its cinema and bowling alley.

O3

The Gold Souk

Location Madinat Zayed Shopping Centre & Gold Souk
Web madinatzayed-mall.com
Times 08:00-23:00 (Daily)
Map 3 p.215

Unfortunately, the more traditional old gold souk burnt down several years ago; to get your hands on glittering goodies now, you'll need to head for the Madinat Zayed Shopping Centre, which is where you'll find the gold centre, or gold souk.

Even without precious metals, the main centre is worth a visit. It has more than 400 outlets selling just about everything, from home accessories to clothing. The quality is as varied, and some of the goods you'll discover are hilarious. But the gold centre, adjacent to the main mall, glitters with the finest gold, diamond and pearl jewellery spread across more than 100 shops. Retailers here base their prices on the daily gold market, so there's no room for bartering, but they also charge for workmanship, and here's where you can do some haggling. Most experts in the art of bargaining reckon that you can get better value for money here than in Dubai's famous gold souk, making it a great place to pick up the traditional souvenir of a pendant with your name engraved in Arabic.

The supervised toddlers' area and the games arcade will also keep the kids entertained. The LuLu hypermarket, open from 08:00 to midnight, makes this a one-stop shopping destination.

Dalma Mall

Location Mussafah **Web** dalmamall.ae
Tel 02 550 6111 **Times** 10:00-22:00 (Sunday to Wednesday),
10:00-00:00 (Thursday to Saturday)
Map 4 p.211

Located off the island in Mussafah, Dalma Mall is a fairly new shopping complex that was built to cater to the residents of Mohammed Bin Zayed City, but has become a favourite destination for anyone living or staying off the island and wanting to avoid battling the downtown traffic.

The mall is anchored by Carrefour, Home Centre, Matalan and one of the country's biggest Marks & Spencer stores – all of which are reasons to visit in their own right. Lovers of the latest fashions will find Dalma Mall to be one of the best places to pick up threads, with all the top international high street brands, like H&M, American Eagle and Topshop, under one roof.

There are also huge offerings from Debenhams and Jumbo Electronics, and a recent addition is Pottery Barn Kids, which is a treasure chest of children's furnishings and bedding.

As for entertainment, there is an international food court that has branches of Soy Express, Koala, Special Juice Bar and Yogen Früz, with seating for 500 visitors. Mall-goers can enjoy blockbusters at the giant 14-screen CineStar Cineplex, while kids will love the FunCity playzone.

Khalidiyah Mall

Location Al Khalidiyah, Al Nahyan Street **Web** khalidiyahmall.com
Tel 02 635 4000 **Times** 10:00-22:00 (Sunday to Wednesday); 10:00-23:00
(Thursday to Saturday) **Map 5** p.215

Not to be confused with the older, smaller Khalidiyah Centre just up the road, Khalidiyah Mall has quickly become one of Abu Dhabi's most popular shopping venues. Located on Al Nahyan Street in the city centre, it is designed in a distinctive Islamic architectural style and is nicely spaced out over three floors.

Home to more than 160 shops, the highlights are department stores such as Debenhams, BHS and Paris Gallery, although there are plenty of choices for visiting fashionistas too, with high street labels like Monsoon and Springfield teamed with a couple of higher-end and more traditional outlets. Sports enthusiasts can turn to the bargain-filled Sports Direct, and other shops sell everything from electronics to accessories and books.

If you get peckish while shopping, the eateries here go a little further than the bog standard food court offerings, with Bricco Café, Cantina Laredo and Chili's offering more

substantial and higher quality fare.

Khalidiyah Mall is particularly popular thanks to its entertainment attractions; the large Sparky's Family Fun Centre includes rides and a bowling alley, while the nine-screen CineRoyal cinema shows all the latest Hollywood flicks.

06

Central Market

Location World Trade Centre Abu Dhabi **Web** wtcad.ae
Tel 800 25327 **Times** 10:00-22:00, some shops close from 13:00-16:00
Map 6 p.215

The World Trade Centre Central Market opened in 2011 and is part of a larger redevelopment of this section of the old city centre that will, eventually, see numerous hotels, residential towers and a mall open in this location.

For the moment, however, Central Market is reason enough to pay this area a visit. The architecture is beautiful, combining elements of traditional Arabia with something altogether more modern to create a maze of wooden hallways and partitions set over two storeys – a modern reinterpretation of the traditional souks that once stood here when Abu Dhabi was in its infancy. The building is dotted with stained glass windows that, when the sun shines through, throw an otherworldly light over the market.

The market is still growing and, although not all of the spaces for its 250 shops and 20 restaurants are yet occupied, there are plenty of eateries to sate the appetites of weary visitors, while the shops here represent arguably the best places for picking up regional artefacts and souvenirs.

10 Other Malls Not To Miss

Al Ain Mall Map 11 p.213
alainmall.net
Al Wahda Mall Map 12 p.216
alwahda-mall.com
Fotouh Al Khair Map 13 p.215
fotouhalkhair.com
Khalifa Centre Map 14 p.216
Tourist Club Area
Mushrif Mall Map 15 p.217
mushrifmall.com
Liwa Centre Map 16 p.215
Markaziya East
Ripe Market Map 17 p.221
ripeme.com
Souk Al Zafarana Map 18 p.213
Al Ain
Boutik Sun & Sky Towers Map 19 p.217
sorouh.com
Multibrand Map 20 p.216
alshaya.com

The Khalifa Street Bridge connects Central Market to the World Trade Centre Mall, home to the Middle East's first House of Fraser, alongside 150 boutiques, an eight-screen cinema, restaurants and cafes, and beautiful outdoor gardens.

Fish, Fruit and Vegetable Souks

Location Al Meena **Times** 04:30 onwards
Map **7** p.226

Fish doesn't get much fresher than
this. The day's catch is loaded onto
the quayside and sold wholesale
for the first two hours of trading
(usually 04:30 to 06:30). Then the
market vendors move on to smaller
quantities after 06:30. If you want
to be munching on the best fish
by lunchtime (there are several
restaurants where the chef will
happily fry up your seafood), then
you'll need to be at the market early.

While the atmosphere is electric, it
is not a place for the faint hearted, as
the smell can be pretty strong. Across
the road from the Fish Souk is the Al
Meena Fruit and Vegetable Souk – a
much more relaxed affair. The price
and quality of the stock is often better
than in the supermarkets but, once
again, arrive early.

Iranian Souk

Location Al Meena Port
Map 8 p.226

It isn't air-conditioned, you won't find any convenient entertainment for the kids, and the facilities are basic to say the least, but if it's a taste of authentic Arabian trading you're after, then the Iranian Souk is the place to go.

Every few days, fresh batches of goods arrive on the dhows or barges from Iran and find their way to these shops. Everything is on sale, from household goods and traditional terracotta urns, to decorative metal, cane and glass items.

The quality of the goods very much depends on how long it has been since the last load came off the boats – get lucky, and you could find some fantastic regional keepsakes or decorative items; if it's been a while, then pickings will be slim indeed.

Bear in mind that the souk is located within a working port and, as such, photography is prohibited. This is also one of the more rough and ready areas – prepare yourself for some sights you may not get at home (like animals in cages). Ladies should dress conservatively and should not explore the souks alone.

> Haggle some more at the Carpet Souk on Al Meena Road, home to Yemeni mattresses and carpets.

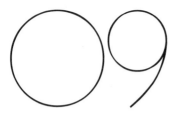

BAS Mall

Location Nr Baniyas Police Station, Baniyas East
Web bawabatalsharq.ae **Times** 10:00-22:00, open until midnight
Thursday-Friday **Map** 9 p.211

The latest addition to Abu Dhabi's retail scene is a true shopper's paradise, consisting of more than 300 shops – including a Carrefour hypermarket that actually has some fun souvenirs, such as Abu Dhabi key rings and traditional shisha pipes.

BAS mall is spread out over two floors, and, as well as fashion staples such as H&M, Springfield and a Centrepoint store, there's a Victoria's Secret and the city's first branch of Gocco – the kids' fashion brand from Spain. You'll also find useful shops like Boots Pharmacy, Ibn Sina Pharmacy and Grand Optics, if you're in need of certain essentials.

Away from the shops, there's plenty more to keep the whole family entertained, like the four-screen Grand Cinemas complex and the Wanasa family entertainment centre, which has a large soft play area, animal-themed carousels and amusement rides. Older children can choose between the 45 high-tech computerised games, an electronic shooting range and five hair-raising funfair rides.

There are 22 food and drink outlets scattered throughout the food court and the rest of the mall, from Thai restaurant Lemongrass and PAUL cafe to Wendy's and Subway. Looking ahead, the mall will include Souk Al Megnas, a traditional souk fashioned in a rich Arabic design, with a variety of locally themed cultural boutiques.

10
Marina Mall

Location Breakwater **Web** marinamall.ae
Tel 02 681 2310 **Times** 10:00-22:00 (Saturday to Wednesday), 10:00-23:00 (Thursday), 14:00-23:00 (Friday) **Map** **10** p.214

Situated out on the Breakwater, but still within easy reach of the Corniche and the city's main hotels, this mall offers a breath of fresh (sea) air to its customers, especially those looking for a mix of familiar western brands with a few individual boutiques and a sprinkling of local goods, particularly on the upper level where you'll find shops specialising in traditional Arabian dress.

Other popular outlets include global favourites, such as Carrefour, Plug-Ins, Sun & Sand Sports and Woolworths. Restaurants, fast food outlets and coffee shops aplenty offer fuel for weary shoppers, while committed bargain hunters should pencil in a couple of visits during the big sale period that lasts from mid-January to the end of February.

If you get bored of shopping, the nine-screen Cinestar complex, Fun City, and the musical fountains near the main entrance will keep you entertained. There's also one of the city's biggest bowling centres and a small ice rink, while those with a taste for heights and views can have a coffee or a bite to eat in the mall's viewing tower.

On the same plot but with a separate entrance is the large Centrepoint department store, where you'll find everything from fashion and baby items to a home and garden shop. Plus, a new addition to the mall is CityStore, which is the region's first stand-alone shop of an English Premium League team. The Manchester City FC shop features a full range of club merchandise.

SOFITEL ABU DHABI CORNICHE

CORNICHE EAST RD, ABU DHABI · UNITED ARAB EMIRATES
TEL: (+971) 2 817 777 · EMAIL: H7507@SOFITEL.COM

The Swimming Pool

Life is Magnifique in Abu Dhabi !

The Suite

SOFITEL
LUXURY HOTELS

AT HOME IN THE PRESTIGIOUS CORNICHE EAST DISTRICT.

ENJOY SOFITEL'S ART DE VIVRE IN A FUTURISTIC ARCHITECTURAL MASTERPIECE
OVERLOOKING THE SEAFRONT. FROM PARIS TO CHICAGO, FROM LOS ANGELES
TO BANGKOK... LIVE A MAGNIFIQUE LIFE AROUND THE WORLD.

WWW.SOFITEL.COM

Destination
Hotels

Yas Viceroy 103

Emirates Palace 104

Desert Islands Resort & Spa 106

Eastern Mangroves 108

Qasr Al Sarab 110

Sofitel Abu Dhabi Corniche 112

Fairmont Bab Al Bahr 113

Hyatt Capital Gate 114

Shangri-La Qaryat Al Beri 116

Westin Abu Dhabi Golf Resort & Spa 119

Hotels

Shangri-La Qaryat Al Beri

Destination
Hotels
Introduction

If there is a single element that has come to define Abu Dhabi city and emirate, it has to be its range of breathtakingly beautiful hotels.

The hotels of Abu Dhabi don't only provide accommodation options and conference facilities, but are in fact the hubs around which the local social scenes revolve. Hotels in Abu Dhabi are places to grab a quick drink; they are where you'll find the best restaurants; and they are idyllic settings to enjoy relaxing by the beach or taking part in a huge variety of activities and watersports.

Today, almost all of the world's leading hotel brands can be found in Abu Dhabi and, given just how significant a role hotels play in the lives of those living in or visiting the region, many of those brands choose the city for showcasing their top hotels, all housed in some of the region's most iconic buildings.

Abu Dhabi has been built on luxurious indulgence as much as the profits of oil and the hotels have come to symbolise that fact. You'll find some of the world's biggest hotels, its most expensive hotels, hotels that straddle golf courses, F1 circuits, mangroves and kilometres of golden sands, as well as hotels that sit on islands which, until just a few years ago, were deserted. The hotels of Abu Dhabi have welcomed kings, queens, heads of government and A-listers from Hollywood and Bollywood.

Whether you are fortunate enough to stay in one of these amazing hotels or have decided to stay elsewhere, you're sure to spend many hours in and around Abu Dhabi's top destination hotels. They are where you'll find some of the emirate's top attractions, bars and restaurants, from the perfect race weekend-views of the Yas Viceroy, to the waterside venues of the Shangri-La Qaryat Al Beri.

The famous Friday brunch (p.181) is a big deal in almost all of these hotels and is a great way to see a hotel or two if you're not staying there. Meanwhile, a number of these hotels sit right on their own private beaches; visitors can usually pay for a day pass that entitles you to spend the day on the beach, relax in the sunloungers, take a splash in the pool and enjoy other facilities. Many also boast family-friendly facilities such as kids' clubs. Desert hotels, meanwhile, can also be enjoyed as a visitor, with most offering luxurious takes on the Bedouin experience, including henna painting, shisha smoking and camel riding, along with traditionally-themed brunches and dinners.

However you choose to enjoy them, do make sure you see as many of Abu Dhabi's stunning destination hotels as you possibly can during your stay here. They truly are some of the city's greatest and most memorable attractions.

One Site Fits All
The Abu Dhabi Tourism Authority portal visitabudhabi.com is a one-stop-shop for hotels, featuring all of the city's main properties and the latest room rates. You can also book rooms through the site.

Yas Viceroy

Location Yas Island West
Web viceroyhotelsandresorts.com
Tel 02 656 0000
Map 1 p.224

Befitting an establishment that first opened its doors for the debut Abu Dhabi F1 Grand Prix in 2009, the Yas Viceroy spans the race track. The two halves of the hotel sit on either side of the track and are connected by a bridge over the track. It is both an architectural classic and an Abu Dhabi icon, especially when the distinctive shell is illuminated at dusk.

The luxurious Viceroy Group has created a hotel that is utterly modern but equally lavish and welcoming. Rooms and suites are vast and all enjoy incredible views over the race track and surrounding Yas Island. The seven restaurants – spanning high-end seafood to luxury Middle Eastern cuisine and sushi – are all individually worth a visit at any time, but especially during race weekends, when diners can watch drivers tackle some of the circuit's most demanding corners. For something truly unique, head to Rush cocktail bar, spectacularly housed in the bridge that spans the race track.

The two rooftop pools and pool bars are otherworldly locations, and the roof is home to the amazing Skylite lounge and club (p.68). There's also a spa, where you can enjoy pampering treatments from the UK's renowned ESPA spa brand.

O2

Emirates Palace

Location Al Ras Al Akhdar **Web** kempinski.com
Tel 02 690 9000 **Map** 2 p.214

Arguably Abu Dhabi's most famous landmark, the $5bn Emirates Palace boasts 392 opulent rooms and suites, all decked out with the latest technology and sumptuous decor. Gold and marble are scattered throughout the hotel, and there are, in total, more than 1,000 chandeliers. If you are feeling lavish, then stay in the Palace Grand Suite, which covers almost 700 square metres and is a bargain at just over Dhs.40,000 per night!

The hotel sits in almost 100 hectares of gardens, which include a private marina, tennis courts, two huge swimming pools, a 1.5km private stretch of sandy beach, and sports pitches.

There is also an opulent Anantara Spa, with one of the country's biggest Turkish hammams, while the hotel has some of the best restaurants, bars and nightspots in the capital.

If you're not lucky enough to stay at Emirates Palace but would still like to soak up its charms, the afternoon high tea is a must. Do book ahead though.

Desert Islands Resort & Spa

Location Al Gharbia,
Sir Bani Yas Island
Web anantara.com
Tel 02 801 5400 **Map** ❸ p.212

Half nature reserve, half luxury resort and spa, Sir Bani Yas Island is the centrepiece of Abu Dhabi's Desert Islands development plan. Today the island is home to the Desert Islands Resort and Spa by Anantara.

Probably one of the most unique resorts anywhere in the world, the Desert Islands Resort is accessible only by boat or by the hotel's private aircraft, which leaves from Abu Dhabi International Airport. Once you arrive, luxurious leisure awaits – from stylish rooms and private beach villas to the wonderful beachside restaurant Samak, and the soothing treatments at the adjacent Anantara Spa.

Back at the hotel, there are swimming pools, tennis courts, archery and a fitness centre, or you can simply relax in the library or browse the traditional-style souk for keepsakes.

Outside the hotel is the Arabian Wildlife Park, where Arabian oryx, giraffes and emus roam freely. Head out on a 4WD safari or a nature walk, or go kayaking to spot the dolphins and turtles that call these waters home.

04
Eastern Mangroves

Location Al Matar **Web** anantara.com
Tel 02 656 1000 **Map** 4 p.217

Located on the east coast of Abu Dhabi island, just 10 minutes from the Corniche in one direction and the airport in the other, Eastern Mangroves Hotel and Spa is Anantara's first city-based hotel in the Middle East. From the traditional Emirati welcome to the elegant but elaborate fixtures and fittings, this is an oasis of tranquility.

Simply look out past the lovely pool to see why it is also a one-of-a-kind destination hotel: the property lies right next to the beautiful mangroves that flank Abu Dhabi island. While the business district may only be a few minutes' drive away, the view here is of nothing but endless water, trees and shrubs – with not a single skyscraper in sight. Many of the rooms, which are luxurious, large and unfussy, share this view.

When you're not relaxing in the resort, there are plenty of leisure activities and facilities on offer, many of which take advantage of the hotel's enviable location within the lush natural environment. There is an on-site marina from which guests can access the local canals for a spot of sailing, kayaking and bird-watching. Alternatively, those in search of active pursuits can also enjoy organised excursions to some of the city's most popular attractions, from horse-riding at the Abu Dhabi Equestrian Club to hitting the green at one of the many excellent golf courses such as the Abu Dhabi Golf Club.

After a day of outdoor adventures, be sure to unwind with a relaxing treat in the resort spa. Anantara is renowned around the world for the quality of its luxurious signature treatments. At Eastern Mangroves, the resort spa menu provides guests with a modern twist on the traditional Turkish hammam.

There is a walkway directly in front of the hotel that leads along the mangroves and right into the city. Better still, you can rent a kayak and explore the mangroves and the marine wildlife from on top of the water.

05

Qasr Al Sarab

Location Liwa **Web** anantara.com
Tel 02 656 1399 **Map** **5** p.212

One of the most sensational wilderness resorts in the world, Qasr Al Sarab Desert Resort by Anantara is an epic citadel deep in the sand-sea hinterland of the Rub Al Khali, or Empty Quarter, the world's largest sand desert. So incredible is the sight of this Arabian fort rising from the ocean of dunes, you would be forgiven for thinking that you'd stumbled onto a Hollywood set. Walled, turreted, scattered with palm trees and featuring giant wooden doors, the main body of the resort sits within one huge complex.

A visit to Qasr Al Sarab is all about complete escape. There is a sensational pool area with a swim-up bar and a variety of day beds just begging to be sprawled across, as guests take in the wonder of the surrounding dunes.

Inside, the luxurious rooms are huge, with oversized bathtubs that merit at least half an hour or so of your downtime. The delicious desert and BBQ restaurants are also deserving of some attention, and the seasonal Bedouin-style dinners are not to be missed.

The spa, which features hammam baths amid peaceful courtyards, is a major focus of the resort. Further afield, the hotel can arrange dune bashing adventures and romantic dinners under the stars.

قصر السراب

QASR AL SARAB

منتجع الصحراء بإدارة أنانتارا
Desert Resort by Anantara

Every moment unveils a
unique story

Tales of rich Arabian traditions at Qasr Al Sarab Desert Resort by Anantara

Surrounded by the vast expanse of dunes and a heritage of centuries inherent to the Liwa Desert, delve into the glorious past of Arabia. Discover a fine blend of contemporary luxuries and a touch of royal opulence. Embark on a voyage of the creation of over a thousand unforgettable moments, cherished and shared for a lifetime.

Design your Arabian adventure now at
anantara.com

Call +971 (0)2 656 1399 or email crome@anantara.com

global hotel alliance

Anantara

Thailand • Indonesia • Vietnam • Maldives • United Arab Emirates • China

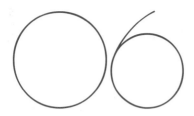

06

Sofitel
Abu Dhabi Corniche

Location Markaziya East **Web** sofitel.com
Tel 02 813 7777 **Map** 6 p.215

From personal service to exquisite finishing touches, the Sofitel offers a touch of class with modern elegance. The spacious rooms ooze comfort and luxurious amenities (even child-sized fluffy bathrobes for little ones), and the stylish bathrooms with rain

showers bring the spa experience to your door. Upgrade to a decadent suite for added extras such as a Nespresso machine, butler, bathroom TV and members' lounge for an exclusive breakfast or drinks.

The spa is an oasis of calm, where the relaxing Swedish massage is sleep-inducing, pure bliss. You can relax by the outdoor pool on the eighth floor, or enjoy free access to the Corniche beach, just a short minibus drive away. By night, indulge in perfectly blended cocktails in the sophisticated Jazz n Fizz, where it's happy hour every day from 17:00 to 22:00. Dining is a feast for the eyes and taste buds – from aromatic Thai to scrumptious afternoon tea, from the finest international dishes to a brunch to end all brunches. Round off the day with shisha and drinks under the stars at the ambient, fire-lit pool bar.

Amazing service and quality seafood shine through at Sofitel's La Mer, home to innovative amuse bouche, freshly caught fish, and signature dishes such as lobster bisque. The sorbet adds a surprising end to a perfect meal.

07

Fairmont Bab Al Bahr

Location Al Maqtaa **Web** fairmont.com/BabAlBahr
Tel 02 654 3333 **Map** **7** p.219

Views of the Sheikh Zayed Grand Mosque, handcrafted delights at the Chocolate Gallery or dining at the phenomenally good Marco Pierre White's Steakhouse and Grill (p.78). There are reasons aplenty to stay at the well-located Fairmont Bab Al Bahr.

Luxurious rooms aside, there's also a collection of stunning outdoor pools overlooking the spectacular creek, as well as a covered children's pool and Jacuzzi. The pool bar is the perfect setting for sundowners, especially during happy hour. The hotel's bars and restaurants are a massive draw, from Italian at Frankie's for romantic dining, to casual al fresco Lebanese at Cedar Lounge. The all-day CuiScene has international appeal.

For the ultimate break, book a Fairmont Gold room to enjoy additional privileges such as Gold Lounge access for breakfast and afternoon tea, a butler on call, and evening drinks and hors d'oeuvres.

Hyatt Capital Gate

Location Al Safarat **Web** hyatt.com
Tel 02 596 1234 **Map** 8 p.218

Hyatt Capital Gate is quite unlike any other hotel in the world. The reason for this singularity is that the hotel is housed in the world's 'most leaning' tower. Climbing 35 storeys, the tower leans 18 degrees from east to west, giving it a total overhang of 33 metres.

The individuality of the structure is beautifully highlighted throughout, from the incredible and hypnotic atrium to the tailor-made furniture that had to be constructed inside the hotel to allow for its unusual lines. The lobby, like the rooms, the restaurant, the spa and the overhanging swimming pool, has huge windows to help guests revel in the location. It is not only unique but also towers above nearby buildings, providing incredible views of the island.

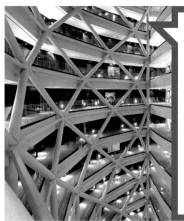

The incredible design flourishes are not just limited to the shape of the tower. The elegant glass facade that sweeps down one side of the hotel actually restricts solar heating of the building, thus cooling it even during the hot months of the Abu Dhabi summer. The hotel houses 189 luxury rooms and suites, which occupy the 18th to 33rd floors. Also, the building has two sets of elevators as the incline is far too steep for one!

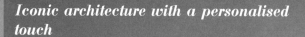

Iconic architecture with a personalised touch

Hyatt Capital Gate Abu Dhabi, a premium hotel in the iconic Capital Gate leans a record-breaking 18 degrees. Enjoy luxury and comfort you have come to expect.

From impeccable dining and superior guestrooms that offer contemporary designs and panoramic views from floor-to ceiling windows, to world class leisure facilities at Rayana Spa, Abu Dhabi's only "sky spa" - a refreshingly elevated oasis!

Strategically located next to ADNEC and within 10-20 minutes drive to the Sheikh Zayed Grand Mosque, the Corniche, Ferrari World, Yas Island and championship golf courses.

Phone: +971 2 596 1234 or email: reservations.capitalgate@hyatt.com.

HYATT CAPITAL GATE ABU DHABI
KHALEEJ AL ARABI ST, PO BOX 95165
T + **(971) 2 596 1234**
F + **(971) 2 596 1235**

abudhabi.capitalgate.hyatt.com
facebook.com/hyattcapitalgate

09
Shangri-La Qaryat Al Beri

Location Al Maqtaa **Web** shangri-la.com
Tel 02 509 8888
Map 9 p.219

The Arabian-inspired architecture and decor of the Shangri-La Qaryat Al Beri are enough to make it a destination hotel of the highest order; however, as well as the superb, luxurious facilties and first-class service, it is the location that makes this hotel really stand out from the pack.

The resort looks out over the narrow creek that separates Abu Dhabi island from the mainland. The 214 spacious rooms and suites capitalise on this unique setting, all boasting private terraces that have stunning sea views out over the creek and to the island, where the Sheikh Zayed Grand Mosque stands majestically. Elsewhere in the hotel, there are two gyms, five swimming pools, and a one-kilometre stretch of private, golden beach.

The spa and outlets – particularly Bord Eau (02 509 8888) and Pearls & Caviar (p.76) – are extremely popular with the city's most fashionable guests and residents looking for an atmospheric night by the water's edge. As if this weren't enough, the Shangri-La has direct access into the Souk at Qaryat Al Beri (p.25), an Arabian-style souk.

Westin Abu Dhabi Golf Resort & Spa

Location Sas Al Nakhl Island **Web** westinabudhabigolfresort.com
Tel 02 616 9999 **Map** 10 p.220

Abu Dhabi has become a top destination for golfing enthusiasts in recent years, and the Westin Abu Dhabi Golf Resort & Spa is a favourite among visitors looking to pursue their hobby during their holiday. If you dream of improving your short game or spending half the day practising your drives, then this hotel will suit you down to a tee. The resort is located right in the middle of the world-renowned Abu Dhabi Golf Club, with its 27-hole championship course, where some of the biggest names in golf come to compete in the Abu Dhabi HSBC Golf Championship each year. Of course, golf is the main attraction, and the hotel can set up everything from tee times to private lessons. But there is also the excellent Heavenly Spa for smoothing out any aches and pains after a round. A lagoon-like main pool, a children's pool and a lap pool are ideal for splashing around in or simply lying next to under the sun.

The hotel's food and drink outlets have an excellent reputation, with the Moroccan-inspired restaurant, Agadir, and the cocktail and wine bar Lemon & Lime (p.74) both attracting visitors from all over the emirates. The Bubbalicious Brunch, held every Friday with a wide range of live cooking stations and free flowing Louis Roederer, is fast becoming the top brunch in the capital.

SOFITEL ABU DHABI CORNICHE

CORNICHE EAST RD, ABU DHABI · UNITED ARAB EMIRATES
TEL: (+971) 2 817 777 · EMAIL: H7507@SOFITEL.COM

The Swimming Pool

Life is Magnifique
in Abu Dhabi !

The Suite

SOFITEL
LUXURY HOTELS

AT HOME IN THE PRESTIGIOUS CORNICHE EAST DISTRICT.

ENJOY SOFITEL'S ART DE VIVRE IN A FUTURISTIC ARCHITECTURAL MASTERPIECE
OVERLOOKING THE SEAFRONT. FROM PARIS TO CHICAGO, FROM LOS ANGELES
TO BANGKOK... LIVE A MAGNIFIQUE LIFE AROUND THE WORLD.
WWW.SOFITEL.COM

Spas

Anantara Spa 125

CHI, The Spa 126

Cristal Spa 127

ESPA 129

Zen The Spa 130

Man/Age 131

Zayna Spa 132

IridiumSpa 133

Mizan 134

Hiltonia 135

Hammam at Eastern Mangroves

Spas
Introduction

Abu Dhabi and luxurious pampering go together like strawberries and cream, or the desert and camels, and you'll find spas of all sizes and styles ready to rub, scrub and knead you into relaxation.

Whether you've just arrived and are in need of a long, lazy day of pampering to help ease you into your vacation, or you have a specific knot that needs to be worked out, someone, somewhere in Abu Dhabi will have the necessary facilities and skills to have you feeling better in no time. Pampering is big business here, from the cavernous spas of the biggest hotels to the beautifying villas of the Bateen area, plus all the smaller, boutique massage centres dotted throughout the city.

There are also numerous massage and relaxation techniques available, with prices and standards varying. The opulent five-star hotels will obviously customise every detail for a blissful experience – and a massage at these usually means you can wallow in Jacuzzis, saunas and steam rooms before and after your treatment – but you'll pay top dollar. Meanwhile, there are plenty of independent places that offer better value for money, but you will have to forego some of the more luxurious facilities. Plenty of hotels have spas pitched somewhere in the middle too.

For a typical Arabian pampering experience, opt for an Oriental hammam. This treatment is traditional in the Middle East region and shares similarities with Turkish baths. The name refers to the bath (the room) in which the treatment takes place – typically an elaborate affair on Abu Dhabi's five-star spa scene. A hammam involves a variety of different experiences, including being bathed, scrubbed and massaged on a hot table. It's an absolute must-do and the hammams at the Anantara spas at the Emirates Palace (p.104) and Eastern Mangroves (p.108) are highly recommended, as is the luxury hammam ritual at Sisters Beauty Lounge (sistersbeautylounge.com).

A number of spas have couples' treatment rooms where you and your significant other can enjoy a massage at the same time. If you're the demanding type, you could even opt for a four hands massage.

For a truly unique Abu Dhabi memory, try something a little different. A number of spas offer unique signature treatments with unusual ingredients. The Westin Heavenly Spa (p.119) has a caviar treatment while, not wishing to be left behind, Mosaic (mosaicspa.ae) offers a crushed olive seed scrub. Treatments at CHI at the Shangri-La (p.126) sound more like a dinner menu, with Arabian date rituals, rose and honey wraps, and Arabic coffee scrubs all available.

Relaxing Prices

Some spas will offer special treatments at certain times of year, as well as reductions on treatments or packages. If you're thinking about indulging yourself, it could also be worth checking out sites like Groupon.com, which often have discounts on spa treatments.

Anantara Spa

Location Emirates Palace **Web** spa.anantara.com
Tel 02 690 9000 **Times** 10:00-22:00
Map 1 p.214

As you would expect of any spa located deep inside the opulent confines of one of the world's grandest and most expensive hotels, the Anantara Spa at the Emirates Palace is the absolute epitome of luxury. Although Anantara's pampering principles were forged and perfected in Thailand, this beautiful spa has been much more heavily influenced by Morocco, with the stunning Moroccan hammam providing the inspiration.

Somewhat surprisingly, perhaps, given its huge surroundings, the spa has just seven treatment rooms, but each is spacious and elegantly kitted out with everything you need for some indulgent me-time. With two steam rooms, two Jacuzzis and a unique ice cave, the facilities are excellent. Treatment highlights include a caviar facial, rejuvenating Elemis massages and the royal hammam ritual.

There are other branches of Anantara spas at Eastern Mangroves (p.108), Qasr Al Sarab (p.110) and the Desert Islands resort (p.106), each of which offers a similar service for guests looking for a bit of luxurious pampering in these stunning spots.

> There are all manner of wraps and scrubs on offer (many using organic local Shiffa products). The Shiffa Emerald Cleansing Ritual is about the most indulgent set of treatments you'll find.

CHI, The Spa

Location Shangri-La Hotel
Web shangri-la.com
Tel 02 509 8900
Times 10:00-00:00
Map 2 p.219

Get the energies flowing at the Shangri-La's CHI spa, a real sanctum of Zen and relaxation. Guests are advised to arrive early to make the most of the facilities, which include a spa pool, steam room, sauna and Jacuzzi – the perfect way to begin the relaxation process before your treatment.

The only real stress is trying to choose from the extensive range of luxurious scrubs, massages, facials, signature treatments and regionally inspired relaxation rituals on offer. The black soap hammam and half-day CHI experiences are particularly recommended for sinking into a state of bliss.

Cristal Spa

Location Cristal Hotel Abu Dhabi **Web** cristalhospitality.com
Tel 02 652 0000 **Times** 10:00-22:00
Map 3 p.215

The UAE is jam-packed with amazing, cavernous spas that could make even the most magnificent mythical palace look a bit on the shabby side. You'd think that, against that kind of backdrop, anything ordinary would struggle to compete, but the fact that the Cristal Spa is not overly fancy is actually where its main appeal lies.

Instead, here you'll find a comfortable lounge area where guests can relax with water or tea, before and after their treatments, along with three nicely-appointed treatment rooms. It's still fairly luxurious – there is a temperature controlled pool, a sauna and Jacuzzi and modern changing rooms – but the focus here is very much on excellent treatments delivered by highly-skilled therapists using organic ingredients. It's this no-frills quality that has many guests returning again and again. Plus, if you're on a flying business visit, you could fit the superb Express Facial into your lunch break.

ESPA

Location Yas Viceroy Abu Dhabi **Web** espaonline.com
Tel 02 656 0862 **Times** 09:00-21:00
Map 4 p.224

The UK brand ESPA has become
something of a byword for luxurious
indulgence and ESPA at Yas Viceroy is
almost the dictionary definition of a
modern, urban spa. From welcome to
goodbye, it's a classy operation, but
not at the cost
of personalised relaxation.

The treatments on offer are
vast – signature treatments, facials,
dedicated male treatments, a
ladies' hammam, and more than 30
massages, wraps and scrubs – while
the range of combination journeys
and 'escapes' offer good value.
In fact, for a top-notch five-star
spa, prices at ESPA remain fairly
reasonable. However, rather than
choosing a therapy 'off the peg', you're
encouraged to provide your therapist
with information about what you
would like, and they'll tailor-make a
treatment for you.

If you've a little extra time
to spare after your spa
treatment, try the intriguing
Metronap – 20 minutes spent
in the space-age recliner
pod is equal to an eight-hour
sleep, apparently.

There are nine treatment rooms,
and the separate male and female
relaxation lounges both overlook the
race track and the marina. The Viceroy
Presidential Treatment Suite features
its own hammam steam room with a
rain shower and colour therapy.

Zen The Spa

Location Beach Rotana Abu Dhabi **Web** rotana.com
Tel 02 697 9000 **Times** 10:00-22:00 (daily)
Map **5** p.216

The Beach Rotana is one of Abu Dhabi's biggest and busiest hotels, located in the bustling Tourist Club

Area; however, descending the stairs down to Zen is like disappearing into a spacious, comfy rabbit hole of relaxation. The uncluttered, minimalist approach provides welcome respite from busy city life.

If you take your pampering seriously, there are a couple of treatment suites available; with private changing rooms, showers and colossal baths, these are luxury defined. Other facilities include lovely relaxation areas.

If it can be scrubbed, wrapped, hydrated, treated or massaged, then it's on the menu at Zen, and signature treatments, such as rejuvenation, immune-boosting, and pregnancy massages, are excellent value. Some of the specialist pampering options include a rasul mud ritual, teen treatments and massage lessons.

Man/Age

Location Marina Mall
Web managespa.com
Tel 02 6818837 **Times** 09:00-22:00
(Saturday to Wednesday), 09:00-
23:00 (Thursday), 14:00-23:00
(Friday) **Map** 6 p.214

Grooming, pampering and preening
are now almost as much of a male
obsession as a female infatuation but,
by and large, the majority of spas are
still female-focused. However, there
are a number of male-only spas that
are changing that and, at the forefront,
is Man/Age.

Located in Marina Mall, it's the
perfect pitstop for weary gents who
lack their other halves' shopping
endurance. Inside, both decor
and atmosphere are unmistakably
masculine. The colour scheme is
brown and burgundy, with plenty of
dark wooden touches, making it feel
like a mix between an old-fashioned
barbers and a gentlemen's club.

While the traditional haircuts
and shaves are available,
the menu here also includes
more metrosexual offerings,
like manicures, pedicures
and facials. There is a range
of no-nonsense massages on
offer – upper body, sports,
deep tissue – as well as a
Moroccan bath and steam
room experience. Treatments
are generally good value with
signature combos offering
particular value for money.

07
Zayna Spa

Location Grand Millennium Al Wahda **Web** millenniumhotels.com
Tel 02 495 3822 **Times** 10:00-23:00 (Daily)
Map **7** p.216

The exotic Asian theme is now so commonplace amongst spas that it's easy to dismiss any place that employs it as just another bog-standard massage joint. Fortunately, there are still spas like Zayna which remind us that Asia is the spiritual home of both the sumptuous spa and seven-star service.

Gentle music, a peppermint aroma and warm south-east Asian hospitality set the scene for head-to-toe pampering. Each of the 10 treatment rooms is fully-equipped with bath and changing facilities. The treatments cover the usual bases,

from luxurious facials to delightful hot stone massages. Signature packages are also available, from 30 minutes up to five hours, ideal for a quick treatment before hitting the beach or a full-blown indulgence day.

Try something new at Zayna: how about a tropical salt mousse glow to restore and re-energise the skin; an aromatherapy hydrating seaweed bath; or even a caviar facial?

Iridium Spa

Location St Regis Saadiyat Island Resort
Web stregissaadiyatisland.com **Tel** 02 498 8888 **Times** 09:00–22:00
Map 8 p.227

As if spending time at one of the Saadiyat Island beach resorts wasn't relaxing enough, Iridium is the chill-out cherry on the calmness cake. The whites, beiges and browns, along with the natural stone and wood finishes used throughout both public areas and treatment rooms, give Iridium Spa an air of rustic perfection. A visit here feels like a woodland retreat as much as a therapeutic treat.

The treatment menu is fairly expansive (although, it is fair to say, Iridium is also on the pricier side) but this spa generally eschews the one-size-fits-all approach to relaxation and therapy. Based on a number of questions, each massage, scrub and wrap is tailored to the client's wants and needs. The therapists are impressively knowledgeable about the treatments, and they do a great job of making you feel utterly relaxed.

09

Mizan

Location Al Maqta Hotel Abu Dhabi
Web roccofortehotelabudhabi.com
Tel 02 617 0000 **Times** 10:00-22:00
Map 9 p.219

In comparison to the major hotel spas such The Ritz-Carlton and Anantara, Al Maqta Hotel's Mizan spa is not particularly well known. In addition, the hotel itself is aimed predominantly at business travellers – again, something that doesn't exactly scream 'top class spa'. So Mizan comes as a real surprise, as this huge spa is one of Abu Dhabi's biggest, brightest and, arguably, best equipped.

The spa has all the usual wet zones, with saunas and Jacuzzis appearing alongside experiential showers, lovely plunge pools, a Vichy shower suite and a deluxe hammam area. The decor throughout the wet areas, ladies' and gents' separate relaxation areas and the private treatment rooms is soft, airy and spacious, creating a pleasant and relaxed mood that differs from the standard spa 'chill out'.

All the usual treatments are covered, from facials to body wraps, although the top-class therapists here perform the basic Thai and Swedish massages so well that it's hard to look past those.

Hiltonia

Location Hilton Abu Dhabi **Web** hilton.com
Tel 02 681 1900 **Times** 09:00-21:00
Map **10** p.214

A long-time favourite amongst the city's residents, the Hiltonia Health Club & Spa is a blissful haven of tranquillity set in some beautiful surroundings. The cool marble floors and ethnic decor make for a consummately soothing setting, and the spacious but well-equipped treatment rooms boast private showers to prep for your treatment or wash off the excess scrubs and oils afterwards.

As well as the aromatherapy and reflexology treatments, which are some of the best and most popular in the city, the spa also offers signature Indian head massages and an intriguing range of hydro treatments, some of which soothe the muscles while others detox the skin and target the main organs.

Alternatively, you can opt for one of the special packages, which combine body treatments with facials and nail care, and include the use of the sauna, eucalyptus steam room and Jacuzzi. The Tropical Bliss (Four Hand Massage) is 90 minutes of pure, well, bliss, and the Cleopatra Hydro Bath and Soothing Massage is an all-over treat.

Wadi Adventure
explore your limits

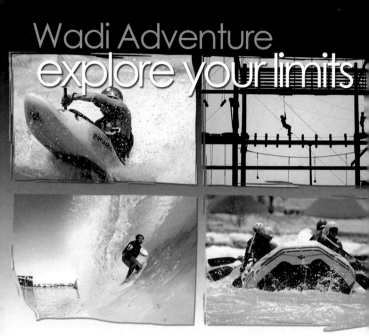

Wadi Adventure is the Middle East's first man made surfing,
whitewater rafting and kayaking destination located in Al Ain.
We also have an airpark, climbing wall and zip line just in case your adventure
needs topping up! With world class activities and
facilities, excellent service and a backdrop like no other, your day can be as
exhilarating or relaxed as you want it to be.
You will also find a family swimming pool and splash pad for our younger
adventurers, as well as a number of food outlets to satisfy a variety of tastes.

WADI ADVENTURE
RAFT • KAYAK • SUI

For enquiries please call us on +971 (0)3 781 842
email: info@wadiadventure.a
www.wadiadventure.a

Adrenaline
Activities

Hot Air Balloon 140

The Yellow Boats 141

Kayaking 142

Formula Rossa 144

Dune Bashing 145

Kitesurfing 146

Spacewalk 147

Yas Marina Circuit 148

Diving 150

Seawings 152

Desert Driving

Adrenaline Activities
Introduction

When it comes to living the ultimate adventure, Abu Dhabi is a complete outdoor playground, with a huge number of experiences on offer.

As ever-increasing tourist numbers demonstrate, Abu Dhabi's appeal is booming with visitors from all over the world stopping in on the emirate to experience just some of what it has to offer. While glitzy malls, breath-taking hotels and gravity-defying buildings may be what many expect when they board the plane, more and more are heading for the UAE to experience some incredible activities and unique experiences. From watersports to motorsports, the choice is endless.

Where some see a vast and hypnotic desert, some people in Abu Dhabi see the world's largest adventure playground, offering sensational experiences like dune bashing (p.05), sand boarding and quad biking, as well as camping and horse or camel riding. One of the best ways to experience a variety of these is on an evening or overnight desert safari (p.178).

To really take in the majesty of the desert, those with a head for heights might like to take to the skies. An early morning hot air balloon ride (p.140) is one enthralling way of doing so, while you can also jump into a small plane to be given a bird's eye tour (p.152) of this island city.

Aside from the desert and the skies, Abu Dhabi's waters also have much to excite thrill-seekers, with activities that range from scuba diving and boat trips (p.141) to high-octane watersports. There are a number of watersports centres such as

Watercooled Abu Dhabi and Hiltonia that provide the full gamut of water-based activities, but you'll also find activity providers at the majority of beachfront hotels.

As well as natural charms, there are plenty of manmade ones too, with the attractions out on Yas Island, arguably providing the highest thrills-per-second ratio you'll find anywhere in the Middle East. And if driving extremely fast sounds more exhilarating, you can try out the performance of an F1 car at the Yas Marina Circuit.

Adrenaline junkies don't need to head out to the desert or jet across to distant shores to get a taste of extreme adventure. There is a myriad of indoor attractions in the capital, which include climbing walls and simulators. Although there is no actual jumping out of planes involved, the indoor skydiving centre at Spacewalk is a thrill-seeking way to enjoy flying in the air for minutes at a time: a giant vertical wind tunnel reproduces the thrilling sensation of jumping from a plane. Plenty, then, to keep even the most ardent adrenaline junkie busy.

Desert Delights

Many of Abu Dhabi's biggest thrills can be found out in the Rub Al Khali, which is also known as the Empty Quarter. This vast desert covers 650,000 square kilometres of towering dunes and sprawling salt flats, making it the world's largest sand desert.

01
Hot Air Balloon

Location Al Ain **Web** ballooning.ae
Tel 04 285 4949 **Times** Approx 05:00–06:00
Price Guide Dhs.995 (Per person) **Map** 1 p.213

Combining soaring skyscrapers, rolling dunes, spectacular islands and beautiful mangroves, Abu Dhabi from the air is an impressive sight. And there's nothing better than taking in the serenity of the desert from a graceful hot air balloon flight.

Balloon Adventures organises tours, with flights departing just before sunrise, although the early start is more than worthwhile once the balloon climbs to provide you with the most awe-inspiring of views.

Of course, you never know where you're going to end up but the support team will be waiting for you with some refreshments once you do touch down, and trips are generally followed by some dune driving as you make your way back.

The Yellow Boats

Location Emirates Palace Marina **Web** theyellowboats.com
Tel 800 8044 **Times** 09:00-17:00 (Daily)
Price Guide Dhs.200 **Map** 2 p.214

If you're after an adrenaline rush on the waters of the Gulf, sign up for a turbo jet experience with The Yellow Boats. They offer exhilaratingly fast-paced tours on board eco-friendly inflatable crafts, which allow you to take in some of the best sights of the Arabian Gulf at heart-stopping speeds.

After heading out from the breakwater and gently cruising past Lulu Island, the captain lets rip and the boat flies over the water past Abu Dhabi icons like Emirates Palace, Marina Mall, and the towers that line the Corniche, making extreme twists and turns along the way. Brace yourself, as you're bound to get a little wet, although the captain does stop at a few choice locations for you to take some holiday snaps.

As well as the Abu Dhabi tours, The Yellow Boats does a high-speed tour of Dubai Marina, if you find yourself in need of an adrenaline fix while visiting the neighbouring city.

> Slow things down a bit and take a leisurely panoramic tour of Dubai Marina by day or night with The Yellow Boats. It costs Dhs.80 for adults and Dhs.30 for children.

O3
Kayaking

Location Shk Zayed Rd, Al Matar **Web** noukhada.ae
Tel 02 650 3600 **Times** 8:00-17:00 (Tuesday to Saturday)
Price Guide From Dhs.150
Map 3 p.218

There's nothing like a breezy morning, soaking up the sun among the mangroves, paddling steadily along while taking in Abu Dhabi's arresting skyline from a whole new perspective. While gliding through the sparkling, turquoise waters of the Gulf, you can admire the city at the same time as exploring Abu Dhabi's stunning coastline with its countless islands and gnarled, watery mangrove forests.

Noukhada Adventure Company offers a variety of fantastic kayaking adventures in single and double kayaks, suited to all levels of experience. It is also committed to eco-tourism principles, so you can be sure that any trip you may take isn't having a negative impact on this amazing environment.

Options start with 90-minute kayak tours of the mangroves where you'll spot fish, birds and turtles, and extend to three-hour island tours, summer full moon tours and BBQ island tours. There are also mystery paddle nights, and two-day expeditions that include a night's stay on one of the islands.

Formula Rossa

Location Ferrari World Abu Dhabi **Web** ferrariworldabudhabi.com
Tel 02 496 8001 **Times** 11:00-20:00 daily except Monday
Price Guide Dhs.195-Dhs.385 **Map** 4 p.224

Imagine a rollercoaster so fast that you have to wear safety goggles. If that sounds like your perfect adrenaline-soaked way to spend a few minutes then imagine no longer, and get yourself to Ferrari World Abu Dhabi. Here, at the world's biggest indoor theme park, you'll find Formula Rossa – the world's fastest coaster. The sensation has to be experienced but the figures tell some of the tale: FR accelerates from 0-100kmph in two seconds, reaching the top speed of 240kmph in 4.9 seconds; riders experience an incredible 1.7Gs of G-Force at some points on the ride; this thrilling ride was modelled on the Ferrari F1 car.

Essentially, the coaster catapults you out and up to a height of 52 metres, before descending through a series of sweeping turns and chicanes that were inspired by the legendary Monza race track in Italy. At 2.2km in total length, Formula Rossa is also one of the longest coasters in the world.

High-octane rides include a 62m high ride that drops vertically through the park's roof, and a flume-style water ride that leads you through a series of twists and turns based on the workings of a Ferrari 599 engine.

O5

Dune Bashing

Location Various
Times Full day or late afternoon
Price Guide Approx Dhs.150-Dhs.350

If one activity sums up the Abu Dhabi adventure experience, it has to be dune bashing. Head out of the city in just about any direction at the weekend, and you'll find scores of locals lined up in their 4WDs about to head off on desert-driving adventures. It's so much fun that both expats and tourists have got in on the act.

For most visitors, the best way to experience a spot of dune bashing is on a desert safari (p.178). The experienced driver will amaze you with just what a 4WD vehicle is capable of doing, as it rocks, rolls, sways and surfs over the dunes in what is effectively a white-knuckle rollercoaster ride but without the rails. Overnight, full day and dune dinner trips are available.

Unfortunately, insurance doesn't cover off-road accidents so you can't just rent a 4WD and give it a go yourself. But, if you still want to get off-road, you can try your hand at quad biking or sand buggying. Many desert safaris offer quadding, while all the main tour operators can also organise a quad bike or buggy tour of the nearby desert, and Al Forsan (p.45) has a dedicated off-road zone and race circuit.

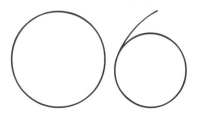

Kitesurfing

Location Various **Web** kitesurfinguae.com
Price Guide Dhs.150 (group lesson), Dhs.300 (private lesson)

Kitesurfing is the most dynamic and exciting watersport on the waves and participation is booming, with kitesurfing set to become an Olympic discipline in 2016. Whether you need to learn the ropes from scratch, want a couple of refresher lessons or are already a pro and simply need to hire some equipment, Abu Dhabi is a great place to try the sport.

There are two main kiting beaches close to the city; one on Yas Island and another at Al Dabayyah, a half hour or so drive west towards Mirfa.

A few hours further west leads you to the Pearl Coast and Mirfa – another great kiting spot. Do note that none of these beaches have facilities or lifeguards, so kiting is always done at your own risk.

There are several individuals and companies in Abu Dhabi that offer kitesurfing lessons, with prices including all the equipment, such as kite, harness and board. Lessons aren't too cheap so, if you're looking to keep the cost down, taking part in small group lessons may be the way to go.

Kitepro Abu Dhabi has a school that covers basic, intermediate and advanced kitesurfing, with all the latest equipment such as radio helmets. Lessons cost Dhs.350 for a 60-minute private tutorial.

07

Spacewalk

Location Abu Dhabi Country Club
Web spacewalk.ae
Tel 02 657 7777
Times 09:00-23:00
Price Guide Dhs.180-Dhs.700
Map 7 p.216

If it's the full skydiving adventure you're after, head over to Dubai where Skydive Dubai offers thrilling tandem jumps over Palm Jumeirah (skydivedubai.ae).

The name of the Abu Dhabi Country Club perhaps conjures images of more leisurely pursuits but, in fact, this is where you'll find one of Abu Dhabi's greatest thrill rides. For anyone who isn't quite ready (or inclined) to jump out of an aeroplane, Spacewalk is the next best thing.

It is not a ride or simulator but an actual indoor skydiving experience, using a giant vertical wind tunnel to reproduce the thrilling sensation of jumping from a plane, but at a fraction of the cost.

For beginners, there's an instructor on hand to help you perfect the technique and alter the wind speed according to your size, weight and ability. However, the experience is such a fun and realistic one that even well-practised skydivers will enjoy the opportunity to perfect some moves thanks to the increased 'free fall' time. Plus, it's a great place for taking funny photos of friends and family whose faces are being distorted by the powerful column of air.

08
Yas Marina Circuit

Location Yas Island West **Web** yasmarinacircuit.com
Tel 02 659 9800 **Times** 09:00-18:00
Price Guide Formula Yas 3000 Experience from Dhs.1500, KartZone
Experience Dhs.55-Dhs.110 **Map** 8 p.224

Ever dreamed of racing alongside Vettel or flying past Alonso on the last bend of a Formula 1 Grand Prix? The Formula Yas 3000 experience gets you pretty close. Yas Marina Circuit offers you the opportunity to strap yourself in for a thrilling race around the track.

After being given a briefing by the fully-qualified instructors, you'll be in charge of the 3000cc V6 racer. Two on-board cameras will capture the action, so that you can take home a reminder of your day.

Yas Marina Circuit has a number of other driving activities available, in cars such as a Chevrolet Camero and Aston Martin GT4. These unique passenger experiences give you the opportunity to feel the pure power and exhilaration of a three-seated drag car (which reaches 100kmph in just two seconds) with a seasoned veteran behind the wheel. The KartZone, meanwhile, offers a fleet of leisure karts that also deliver an excellent racing experience, perfect for families and groups.

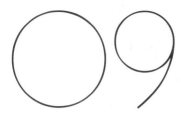

Diving

Location Marina Al Bateen Resort **Web** arabiandivers.net
Tel 050 614 6931 **Times** Various
Price Guide Various
Map 9 p.215

The warm seas and clear, calm waters of the Arabian Gulf are perfect for exploring the region's varied underwater life, and the seas around Abu Dhabi's numerous islands have a fair amount of marine creatures to discover. There are also plenty of interesting dive sites, especially wrecks, some of which are within easy reach of Abu Dhabi.

Local dive companies can get you out to these sites, as well as help you improve your diving skills, with courses offered under the usual international training organisations.

Arabian Divers & Sportfishing Charters, based in Al Bateen Marina, is one of the best known companies, with more than 20 years of experience off the coast of Abu Dhabi. As well as the boats and equipment, the company has a classroom and training pool, so even if you've never dived before arriving in Abu Dhabi, you could leave with a PADI qualification and a couple of dives in the Arabian Gulf under your diver's belt. The company also organises big game sport fishing trips throughout the year.

10

Seawings

Location Various **Web** seawings.ae
Tel 04 807 0708 **Times** Various
Price Guide From Dhs.995

It may only be for the most stout-hearted of tourists, but there's no denying that flying is one of the best ways to soak up the awe-inspiring skyline that Abu Dhabi has become famous for.

The Seawings Abu Dhabi Pearl package flies across the city, providing views of Abu Dhabi's most iconic landmarks, including Ferrari World, Yas Marina Circuit, Abu Dhabi Corniche and Emirates Palace. After landing in the waters of Yas Island, you can visit Ferrari World free of charge for even more thrills. It's an absolutely stunning experience and one you won't forget in a hurry.

The other option is the Dubai Classique package, which takes in the amazing Abu Dhabi sights before heading to Dubai and giving aerial panoramas of Dubai Marina, Burj Khalifa and Palm Jumeirah. After the 40-minute trip, you are free to explore the sights of Dubai.

Helicopter tours are increasingly popular too and Falcon Aviation Services (falconaviation.ae) provides chopper tours over the UAE capital and its main landmarks. If you're feeling extravagant, you can charter a seaplane or helicopter and its captain by the hour and set out your own dream route.

BAKE
ABU DHABI'S
SUNLOUNGE
DESTINATION

Saadiyat public beach

Abu Dhabi beaches at Corniche

DAILY RATES AS LOW AS AED 25
MEMBERSHIPS AVAILABLE

Al Bateen beach

FOR MORE INFORMATION AND DIRECTIONS VISIT:
www.BAKEuae.com
f www.facebook.com/BAKEUAE @BAKEuae

Places In
The Sun

On The Water 158

BAKE on Saadiyat Beach 160

Family Park 161

Coast Roads 162

Al Maya Island Resort 164

Fairmont Bab Al Bahr Beach Club 165

The Desert 166

Breakwater 168

Capital Park 169

Monte-Carlo Beach Club 170

Sun

Beachside Watersports

Places In
The Sun
Introduction

Abu Dhabi has no shortage of places for beachgoers
to head to in order to top up their tan, or for outdoor
enthusiasts to enjoy the year-round sunshine.

During the cooler months, there are some excellent outdoor options to discover across Abu Dhabi. In fact, there are so many alfresco delights, you might be tempted to never step inside a mall or a hotel during the winter. The green parks are superbly maintained, while the beaches draw crowds of sunbathers and swimmers, particularly at weekends. But that's not all; there's plenty of fun to be had beyond the city limits too. And, even though you're unlikely to tire of enjoying the urban attractions, there are a couple of huge adventure playgrounds – in the form of the desert and the Arabian Gulf – just waiting to be explored.

There's no doubt that Abu Dhabi's beaches are some of the main attractions for sun-seeking visitors. Blessed with warm weather, calm ocean waters and long stretches of sand, the emirate's beaches come in various types, depending on requirement. Choose from public beaches (limited facilities but no entry fee), the Corniche beach parks (good facilities and a nominal entrance fee), or private beaches (normally part of a hotel or resort). Regulations for public beaches are quite strict, but that's not necessarily a bad thing. Dogs are banned, for instance, and so is driving, therefore the sand is kept clean. Other off-limit activities include barbecues, camping without a permit and holding large parties.

Abu Dhabi is also home to a number of excellent parks, with lush green lawns and a variety of trees and shrubs creating the perfect escape from the concrete jungle of the city. Most have a kiosk or cafe selling snacks and drinks, and some have barbecue pits. Remember, these get particularly busy over the weekend.

Regulations at parks vary, with some banning bikes and rollerblades, or limiting ball games to specific areas. Some parks have a ladies' day when entry is restricted to women, girls and young boys.

What *Not* To Wear

Compared to the rest of the GCC, Abu Dhabi is a fairly liberal city that adopts a much more relaxed attitude to what visitors can wear in public. However, there are some rules that apply to dress and beachwear that visitors must follow. Bikinis are fine in private hotel resorts, although string bottoms and going topless is a big no-no – wherever you are in Abu Dhabi. While plenty of beachgoers wear bikinis on public beaches, it can occasionally attract unwanted attention, so best to wear a one piece or sarong while sunbathing or head for a beach park or resort beach. For men, it is worth remembering that some nationalities (and the fashion police) might find Speedos offensive, and avoid going to a nearby cafe or shop without putting a t-shirt on first or you'll be considered rude.

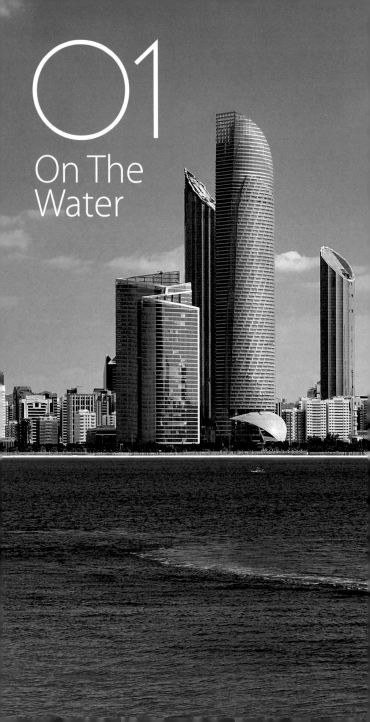

O1

On The
Water

With a stunning coastline, calm seas and year-round warm waters, a day out on a boat should appear on any explorer's itinerary. There are several options; from a day of sailing around the islands, to an evening cruise along the Abu Dhabi Corniche – and all of them are wonderfully atmospheric experiences.

Some companies run regular, scheduled trips onboard boats that range from high-speed RIBs to luxurious catamarans serving BBQs and playing music on board. Others charter out boats to private parties for sailing, sightseeing or even fishing trips.

For something a bit different, head to the port area where you can find numerous traditional dhows lined up. Some of these no longer transport goods across the Arabian Gulf but instead combine evening sightseeing tours with Arabian cuisine and onboard entertainment, making for a unique evening out. Companies operating out of Abu Dhabi include Belevari Marine (belevari.com), ART Marine (artmarine.net) and Ocean Active (oceanactive.com).

BAKE on Saadiyat Beach

Location Saadiyat Public Beach, Saadiyat Island
Web BAKEuae.com **Times** 08:00-20:00
Price Guide Sun lounger Dhs.50 (Weekdays), Dhs.75 (Weekends)
Map 2 p.227

As you walk along the jetty to Saadiyat Public Beach, put your toes into the pristine white sand and gaze across to the turquoise waters of the Arabian Sea. And then relax.

This heavenly stretch of beach is all yours to enjoy in luxury beach club style – but without the price tag. Managed by BAKE, you can rent sunloungers with umbrellas for the day, as well as lockers (Dhs.15) and towels (Dhs.10). There are showers, changing rooms and a small shop selling beach essentials, with plans for a beach cafe and non-motorised watersports. Lounge in the sun, bathe in the shallow warm sea, walk along the beach or work out at the weekly beach yoga classes. There are even Oryx roaming the dune grasses and turtles nesting from May to October. For the ultimate indulgence, pop into the neighbouring Park Hyatt for lunch.

For stylish sun-worshipping visit BAKE's Abu Dhabi Corniche hangouts – at Al Sahil Beach and Family Beach Gates 2 and 3. Facilities include sunloungers, day beds, cabanas, towels and showers. Perfect for sunsets.

Family Park

Location Corniche Road
Price Guide Free
Map 3 H2 P1

Pedal along tree-lined walkways, picnic in the sun, or explore the themed play areas. There are many reasons why Family Park, located along Corniche Road, has become a firm favourite with parents and children alike.

Green areas are set in a landscape of wide walkways, tunnels, water features and landscaping, just minutes from the beach and Corniche. There are age-specific play zones scattered across the park, including a pirate ship, toddler village with toy train and fire engine, and swings, slides and tunnels of all shapes and sizes. The Misty Valley Walk is great fun! Light refreshments are served at a central cafe, and there are plenty of shaded grassy areas and picnic spots to enjoy an ice cream or a BBQ.

The park really comes to life for the Let's Go Summer festival, held every June-July. There is a wide range of sports activities and water games such as the 3D Shark Bite and Banzai 20ft Rip Curl Curve water slides, as well as soap soccer.

04

Coast Roads

Location Eastern Ringroad to Coast Road
Map 4 p.217

Abu Dhabi island is flanked by the Eastern Ringroad on the north east side and the Coast Road on the south west. You may not expect two of the main arteries connecting the foot of the island with the Corniche and central business district to provide nice outdoor areas. However, just off the sides of these roads – both of which enjoy delightful coastal views – the land has been developed to provide long green strips with barbecue areas, play areas and walking paths.

The coastal flank of the Eastern Ringroad, which looks out over the mangroves, eventually meets the Eastern Mangroves Hotel and Spa by Anantara, where a public path follows the water all the way into town – a great place for a long walk. On the other side of the island, the road leads past the Al Gurm Resort before arriving at Al Bateen Marina.

Al Maya Island Resort

Location Halat Al Bahraini (Al Maya Island) **Web** almayaislandresort.ae
Tel 02 667 7777 **Map** 5 p.212

Al Maya Island Resort is a real undiscovered gem of Abu Dhabi. Located just nine kilometres from the Corniche, you can jump on board a boat at one of the main marinas and be on Al Maya Island in less than 15 minutes. If you do just that, you'll find a beautiful boutique resort at the other end. Operated by Abu Dhabi Country Club, there are just six villas and five chalets at the resort, as well as a lagoon-like swimming pool, a restaurant and a watersports centre which offers banana boating, kayaking, wakeboarding, paddle boarding and scuba diving.

Families and couples will both enjoy either a day or a few days at Al Maya, but the island's main appeal is for younger holidaymakers – or at least the young at heart. On select Fridays throughout the year, boats leave the Al Maya jetty behind Rotana Khalidiyah Palace and take up to 1,500 partygoers out to the island for afternoon beach and pool parties.

06

Fairmont Bab
Al Bahr Beach Club

Location Al Maqtaa **Web** fairmont.com/BabAlBahr
Tel 02 654 3333 **Times** 06:00-22:00 (daily)
Map 6 p.249

The beach club at Fairmont Bab Al
Bahr Beach Club is without doubt
one of the best around. The single
day rate entitles guests to more than
the stretch of immaculate beach,
which overlooks the main island and
Sheikh Zayed Grand Mosque, with its
comfortable range of loungers and
recliners; you can also take a dip in the
two temperature-controlled pools, lap
pool or laze in the poolside Jacuzzi.

You can try your hand at beach
football, badminton, Frisbee, softball,
volleyball, rugby and even beach
bocce. There are also kids' pools and
play areas, trampolines, and organised
sandcastle building. Throw in the
poolside bar and restaurant, and it's
easy to while an entire day away here,
soaking up the sun.

07
The Desert

With vast areas of virtually untouched wilderness right the way across the UAE, taking to the desert is a very popular pastime. Every other vehicle on Abu Dhabi's roads seems to be a 4WD but, unlike in many countries where they're reserved for running the kids to school, there is ample opportunity to truly put them to the off-road test in Abu Dhabi.

Dune bashing, or desert driving, is one of the toughest challenges for both car and driver, but, once you have mastered it, it's also the most fun. Those who want to drive themselves should do so in a controlled environment, such as OffRoad Zone (offroad-zone.com) which is at Jebel Ali, on the way to Dubai; here, you can practise tackling all manner of obstacles.

If you don't know where to start, or don't want to risk driving yourself, then you should contact one of Abu Dhabi's many tour companies that offer desert and mountain safaris (p.178). These desert safaris are great ways to spend time out there amongst the Arabian sands – daytime safaris combine dune bashing with quad biking, camel riding and lunch, while evening safaris add huge buffets and traditional entertainment to the mix. Some even allow you to camp out beneath the stars.

Breakwater

Location Corniche **Map** 8 p.214

Jutting out from the south west end of the Corniche is the Breakwater where you'll find Marina Mall, but it also provides numerous opportunities for enjoying the fresh air and bright sunlight. For starters, the Breakwater is a great place to go for a stroll, with wide pavements and plenty of places to stop and watch the fishermen who are casting into the Gulf.

Both Abu Dhabi International Marine Sports Club (adimsc.ae) and the Heritage Village (p.16) make for interesting stops as you walk out to the end of the Breakwater where the giant flagpole stands tall. Marina Cafe and Havana Cafe are located en route, giving you the opportunity to grab a drink and take some great snaps of the view back to the Corniche and the towers that line it.

Finally, if you head up to the west side of Marina Mall, you'll come to Mirage Marine – a Lebanese cafe with a delightful outdoor area where you can eat mezze, smoke shisha and spot dolphins in the lagoon between the Breakwater and Emirates Palace. Above Mirage Marine is Il Porto – an Italian restaurant with a cracking terrace that is also a top alfresco offering.

The Abu Dhabi Theatre building is also worth a look: its shape led to speculation that it was either a mosque or an observatory. It has now fallen into disuse, but stands next to a towering 123m tall unsupported flagpole.

Capital Park

Location Khalifa Street, Markaziya East **Web** adm.gov.ae
Times 0800-2300, closed on Fridays
Price Guide Dhs.1, free for children below 10 **Map** 9 p.215

This recently-refurbished park is a welcome green patch of tranquillity in the middle of the bustling city centre. Each little cove of the garden has a small selection of climbing frames, swings and slides, while there's a horse and cart that takes younger children for small trips around the park. The large pond in the centre of the park erupts periodically with bursts from the stunning fountains, taking visitors by surprise.

Elsewhere, the park has plenty of shaded areas under mature trees. This may not be the kind of place where you would spend the day, but it's nice for a quick pit stop, a picnic or BBQ lunch, or simply an evening walk.

Vending machines and an enclosed cafe provide simple refreshments – and there is a popular takeaway pizza place right across the road. There is also a small mosque and a municipal plant shop.

10
Monte-Carlo Beach Club

Location Saadiyat Island **Web** montecarlobeachclub.ae
Tel 02 656 3500 **Price Guide** Day pass from Dhs.400
Map 10 p.227

The best way to think of Monte-Carlo Beach Club is as a five-star hotel without the bedrooms; walking into the magnificent lobby, guests are greeted as though they're checking into a luxury beach resort. Also inside, you'll find a fully-equipped gym, a coffee lounge, a restaurant and a couple of bars. The changing rooms and wet areas include a palatial Jacuzzi, sauna, steam room and day beds for a bit of a snooze or a spot of reading.

But the real action is outside the giant lobby windows. Firstly, there's an amazing stretch of wild beach, with the warm waters of the Gulf lapping up on to the sands. Then there is the huge pool, surrounded by sumptuous, sprawling cabana-style day beds, as well as comfortable luxury sun loungers.

If all those outdoor hours start to wear you down, you can head to Le Deck (p.57) for sustenance, or snacks and drinks can be delivered to wherever you're relaxing. Kids should love it too; there's a children's pool, as well as a kids' club for those aged between three and 12.

Abu Dhabi
Experiences

The Corniche 176
Desert Safari 178
Friday Brunch 181
Shisha 182
Boat Racing 183
Big Bus Tours 184
Yas Island Concerts 185
Dhow Dinner Cruise 186
Championship Golf Courses 188
Architecture 190

Experiences

Abu Dhabi Experiences
Introduction

The once sleepy pearling village has been transformed into a modern metropolis. This new global icon is an intoxicating place filled with experiences to match.

Many of Abu Dhabi's most ambitious projects are now recognised all over the world, from the majestic Emirates Palace (p.104) and the spectacular Aldar HQ 'Pill' building to the awesome Yas Island. Abu Dhabi is a byword for luxurious indulgence, multicultural lifestyles, architectural excess, lavish beach holidays and general fun in the sun, but it is also gaining a reputation for being one of the most diverse tourist destinations on the planet; a place where your appetite can be sated, whether you're into relaxed beach holidays, cultural breaks, activity trips or sporting tours.

And while Abu Dhabi may be many things to many people, there are a few specific activities and experiences that are either unique to the UAE capital, or perfectly sum up a side of the city. The juxtaposition of old and new, the mix of traditional Arabia with the West, is one characteristic that baffles, intrigues and delights visitors and, with that in mind, the various bus (p.184) and boat tours (p.141) provide the perfect perspective to take in this contrast. Being in a traditional souk one moment and a sprawling mall the next is pure Abu Dhabi.

While you're in the mood for touring, a desert safari (p.178) – which usually comes complete with an Arabian buffet, entertainment and dune bashing – is the kind of experience you'll struggle to find elsewhere; hot air ballooning (p.140) may be available in other locations, but doing it as the sun rises over the desert is pretty special.

In terms of modern Abu Dhabi, you'll want to spend some time in the Corniche area, which is home to the beach parks, Etihad Towers (etihadtowers.com) and the Breakwater. But dominating the Corniche is, of course, Emirates Palace and looking out from the terrace of the world's most expensive hotel while sipping on gold-trimmed coffee is an experience that is only available in Abu Dhabi – until someone builds a more expensive and opulent hotel, of course!

Overindulgence is undeniably an Abu Dhabi trait too and there's no doubt that residents and visitors in the city enjoy the finer things in life. Brunch (p.181) may be available around the world, but the Abu Dhabi brunch is something else entirely. Meanwhile afternoon tea in the city has all the old world charm you'd expect to find in London or Paris, rather than a city in the Middle East.

Taste of Arabia
Tucking into traditional mezze and grilled meats, washing it all down with a fresh fruit juice and finishing your meal with a shisha pipe may not be unique to Abu Dhabi, but it is pure Arabia and the UAE capital has some of the best places to enjoy that traditional experience.

01

The Corniche

Location Al Khubeirah
Map 1 p.215

The Corniche is the beating heart of the capital, connecting the west of the island to the east of the island but also demarking its main business and tourism areas – it's an area to soak up the charm and atmosphere of modern Abu Dhabi. It's a lovely place for a stroll but the whole Corniche runs some eight kilometres in total; if you want to enjoy the entire length of it, take advantage of the waterfront section which is fully paved, making it ideal for rollerblading, jogging or cycling; bikes are available to hire near the Hiltonia Beach Club (p.135).

The Corniche Road is lined with the high-rise towers that make up Abu Dhabi's spectacular skyline. The inland side has been beautifully landscaped with parks, small gardens, fountains and covered seating areas that are perfect for a picnic. All areas are easily accessible, with parking and safe pedestrian underpasses.

At the western end, towards the Emirates Palace, a multimillion dirham project has modernised the swimming beaches and introduced a range of cafes along the shoreline.

O2
Desert Safari

Location Various
Times 15:00-21:00 (Daily)
Price Guide Around Dhs.250 (Adult)

You can go almost anywhere and lie on a beach, laze by the pool, take to the shops and dine at high-end restaurants – what makes a trip to Abu Dhabi truly special are the kinds of experiences that are totally unique to this region. Desert safaris certainly fit that bill.

All of the main tour operators offer very similar packages and you should be able to book directly with your hotel. For the full Arabian experience, book an evening safari – you'll be picked up in a 4WD from your hotel before being whisked away into the desert, where your experienced driver will show you exactly what off-road vehicles were made for.

After the rollercoaster 4WD ride, you'll stop on one of the tallest dunes to watch the sun go down over the vast desertscape. There's time to take your next Facebook profile picture, before you get back into the vehicle to go to a Bedouin-style desert camp. There, you can ride a quad bike, mount a camel, have your hands painted with henna, smoke shisha, feast on an Arabian banquet, and enjoy the entertainment – in the form of a belly dancer and a whirling dervish dancer. Finally, pile into the 4WD for the journey back to your hotel.

Friday Brunch

Location Various **Times** 12:00-16:30
Price Guide Dhs.95-695

You might think the word 'brunch' is self-explanatory: a portmanteau of 'breakfast' and 'lunch' – a meal you have between the two more accepted dining anchors. If so, you clearly haven't had brunch in Abu Dhabi. Far from the genteel image of croissants, scrambled eggs and coffee over the day's papers, brunch in Abu Dhabi is synonymous with triumphantly eating your own body weight in food and washing it down with free-flowing champagne. And all for a set price.

The Tavern, Belgian Beer Cafe and Heroes are the spiritual homes of the debauched brunch, while Choices and CuiScene are both child-friendly options, offering smaller portions and a less alcohol-orientated atmosphere; Jing Asia offers something a bit different. Bubbalicious at The Westin and Olea at St Regis epitomise Abu Dhabi's posh and pricey all-inclusive approach; Origins at Yas Viceroy and the brunch at Pearls & Caviar are equally high-minded affairs.

Shisha

Location Various cafes and restaurants **Price Guide** Dhs.50-200

Smoking the traditional shisha (water pipe) is a popular pastime enjoyed throughout the Middle East. Also known as hookah or hubbly bubbly, it is usually savoured in a local cafe while chatting with friends. Shisha pipes can be smoked with a variety of aromatic flavours, such as strawberry, grape or apple, and you'll know when you're walking past a shisha cafe thanks to the sweet scent floating on the breeze. The experience is unlike normal cigarette or cigar smoking as the smoke is 'smoothed' by the water, creating a much more soothing effect, although smoking shisha does still cause health problems.

Just as popular is the practice of drinking fruit juices, with many traditional Middle Eastern cafes and restaurants serving up even more flavours of freshly-squeezed juices than they have of shisha tobacco; and the two go hand in hand quite nicely. Arguably the best place in town to get shisha and juice is Tarbouche's Central Market branch. The roof terrace is always alive and buzzing with people drinking fruit cocktails and enjoying their hubbly bubbly.

05
Boat Racing

It's maybe not the most obvious or globally-popular of spectator sports, but boat racing is an important part of Emirati culture, reflecting the country's close connection with the sea. If you do get the chance to watch, some fantastic racing takes place in Abu Dhabi.

With both the Abu Dhabi Grand Prix in November and then the Dubai Grand Prix in December, the UAE is the only country with two stops in the Class 1 World Power Boating Championship (class-1.com). These boats are something to behold, reaching speeds of 250km/h and sometimes barely even touching the water.

In addition to Class 1 events, there is the F1 Abu Dhabi Grand Prix, the Wooden Power Boats Championship, the UAE Jet Ski Championships

(see adimsc.ae for all those events), sailing competitions and dhow races throughout the year at the Abu Dhabi International Marine Sports Club.

For something completely different, however, every year there's the Dubai Dragon Boat Festival (dubaidragonboat.com) in April, with teams from all over the UAE competing in the races.

In January 2012, Abu Dhabi was the first Middle East port ever to host the world's biggest sailing event, the Volvo Ocean Race, which drew huge crowds. The capital will host the third 2014/15 Volvo Ocean Race stopover in December 2014.

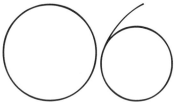

Big Bus Tour

Location Various **Web** bigbustours.com
Tel 800 244 287 **Times** 09:00-17:00 (Daily)
Price Guide Dhs.200 (Adult)

If you only booked a short break in Abu Dhabi, or perhaps are stopping in for a few days en route to another destination, then you'll want to see as much of this incredible city as possible in a short amount of time. A bus tour is an excellent option for seeing all the highlights in one go.

The Big Bus Tour is arguably the pick of the tours; providing bus tours of 12 cities around the globe, from Budapest to Shanghai, this hop-on hop-off tour knows exactly what tourists want to see from its modern fleet of air-conditioned double-deckers, as well as just what they want to hear on the commentary track.

Marina Mall is the main starting point in Abu Dhabi, but riders can get on or off at any of the 11 stops that include Sheikh Zayed Grand Mosque, the Meena souks, the Corniche, Saadiyat Island, Central Market, the Public Beach and Heritage Village. Abu Dhabi Mall is the ideal lunch time stop, with its range of 40 food outlets.

The ticket, which is valid for 24 hours, includes free entry to the Sky Tower viewing platform at Marina Mall, as well as a shuttle bus out to Yas Island. The Big Bus Company also offers a combined Abu Dhabi/Dubai ticket so that you can explore both cities in two days.

07

Yas Island Weekends

Location Yas Island West
Web yasisland.ae **Map** 7 p.224

The entertainment on Yas Island began with the series of F1 concerts that still accompany the Grand Prix each November and have seen the likes of stars such as Eminem, Britney Spears, Paul McCartney, Kylie Minogue, Nickelback, Aerosmith, Beyonce, Kanye West, Linkin Park and Prince play over the years.

However, the concerts proved so popular that the organiser, Flash Entertainment, has rolled out other similar events throughout the rest of the year, under the title of Yas Island Show Weekends. Although some parts of the weekend sometimes take place elsewhere, the majority are focused on the du Arena – a state-of-the-art concert pavilion that sits between two of the arms of Ferrari World. The venue even features a cooling system that allows events to be held in the summer months.

Although other events, such as drag racing and basketball, have formed part of the weekends before, they're traditionally music-focused, with Stevie Wonder, Snoop Dogg, Madonna and Shakira all having performed here.

The Yas Island hotels offer special discounted rates on concert dates; attractions like Ferrari World and Yas Waterworld usually follow suit, making for an action-packed weekend of non-stop fun and entertainment.

08

Dhow Dinner Cruise

Location Various
Times 19:30- 22:30 (Daily)
Price Guide Dhs.120-345

One of the absolute Abu Dhabi must-do experiences for tourists is the dhow dinner cruise, which takes visitors out from the dhow harbour at the eastern end of the Corniche and sails them along the length of the Corniche.

Traditionally trading crafts that ship cargo between the Gulf and Iran, these dhows have been converted to become floating restaurants; the two to three-hour tours typically see diners sit on the top deck, beneath the stars, while an Arabian buffet is served up. Food such as Arabic mezze and mixed grill platters are traditional fare, followed by a dessert of fruit and local sweets.

The cruises take in all the traditional landmarks of the Corniche, giving guests a unique view of the distinctive city skyline. See the domes, towers, and minarets that line the Corniche Coast road, while relaxing at your table or on floor cushions.

Dhow sunset and lunch cruises are also available.

09
Championship Golf Courses

Location Various
Times 06:00-22:00 (Daily)
Price Guide Dhs.260-695 (18 holes)

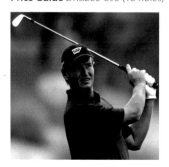

With big names like Gary Player, Peter Harradine and Kyle Phillips all lending their star-power to Abu Dhabi's greens through successful design collaborations, it is little surprise that the popularity of the city as a world-class golf destination has now been cemented. Clubs and societies from all over the world are making the golf tour to Abu Dhabi an integral part of their annual schedules. And the golf is varied; from championship courses to links and beach courses, and even a sand course.

Hotels and tour operators can pre-book your tee times if you're heading over for a golf-heavy few days, or you can contact the courses directly. If you stay at certain hotels, such as the Westin Abu Dhabi Golf Resort & Spa or the hotels on Yas and Saadiyat, you can book packages that include a round or two as well as your room.

Top Ten
Golf Courses

Saadiyat Beach Golf Club
Map **11** p.227
sbgolfclub.ae
Yas Links Map **12** p.224
yaslinks.com
Abu Dhabi Golf Club
Map **13** p.220
adgolfclub.com
Abu Dhabi City Golf Club
Map **14** p.216 *adcitygolf.ae*
Emirates Golf Club Map **15** p.213
dubaigolf.com
Dubai Creek Golf & Yacht Club
Map **16** p.213
dubaigolf.com
Jumeirah Golf Estates Map **17** p.213
jumeirahgolfestates.com
Montgomerie Golf Club
Map **18** p.213
themontgomerie.com
The Els Club Map **19** p.213
elsclubdubai.com
Al Badia Golf Club Map **20** p.213
albadiagolfclub.ae

> You may like to time your golf trip to coincide with the Abu Dhabi HSBC Golf Championships (abudhabigolfchampionship.com), a real hit with fans and merrymakers alike.

10
Architecture

If the name 'United Arab Emirates' has come to stand for any one thing, it is surely architectural excess. While cities across the rest of the world demand practicality of their builders, in Abu Dhabi, architects are encouraged to let their creativity run wild.

In the past, the architectural masterpieces to hit the capital have been bound by a sense of Arabian traditionalism, not that this has prevented either Emirates Palace or Sheikh Zayed Grand Mosque from becoming modern icons of the Middle East. Now, however, Abu Dhabi's most interesting buildings are absolutely modern and bound only by what is and isn't possible.

If you're in the mood for an architectural tour de force, start at the western end of the Corniche with the $5bn Emirates Palace and contrast it with the neighbouring Etihad Towers – the complex of five uber-modern glass skyscrapers that glisten against the blue skies above.

While you're in the mood for stylish skyscrapers, head to the south of the island; there, you'll find a world record breaker high above the vast ADNEC conference centre: Capital Gate is officially the world's most leaning tower, with an 18° slant. Nearby is the recently-opened Sheikh Zayed Bridge. This snaking bridge is the third bridge connecting the south of the island with the mainland and was designed by Iraqi-British architect Zaha Hadid.

Off the island, the spherical Aldar HQ (below) – known as 'The Pill' – has to be seen to be believed. And the Guggenheim and Louvre museums on Saadiyat Island are sure to amaze when they open in 2015.

You can see several stunning buildings off the main island too. One such icon is the futuristic Yas Viceroy hotel (far left), which glows blue at night and straddles Yas Marina Circuit; it has become one of the most famous structures in sport today.

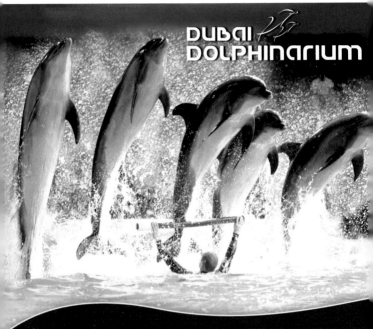

DUBAI DOLPHINARIUM

Dolphin and Seal Show

Get up close and personal to graceful bottlenose dolphins and playful northern fur seals. A 45-minute interactive extravaganza showcases these amazing animals' astounding skills. Wet wild and totally wonderful!

Show Times

Mon, Tue, Wed, Thu : 11am & 6pm
Fri & Sat : 11am, 3pm & 6pm

Swimming with Dolphins

Make your visit truly memorable with a group or private swim session.
Mon to Thu - 1pm to 4pm

Location: Creek Park, Gate 1, Dubai, Call: +971 4 336 9773
Toll Free: 800-DOLPHIN (800-3657446)
www.dubaidolphinarium.ae

Our Vision: To Create an excellent city that provides the essence of success and comfort of living.

Outside Of
Abu Dhabi

Hatta 196

Oman 197

Dubai 199

Al Ain 202

The Pearl Coast 203

Liwa 205

Fujairah 206

Northern Emirates 207

Emirates National Auto Museum 208

Al Maha Desert Resort & Spa 209

Beyond

Beyond

Dubai Skyscrapers

Outside Of
Abu Dhabi
Introduction

From the vast Rub Al Khali desert in the south, to the majestic Hajar Mountains in the north, there's an incredible country to visit outside of Abu Dhabi's city limits.

Abu Dhabi may have everything from sports and souks to boutiques and beaches, but there are a number of interesting and varied areas outside of the city borders too; the other emirates in the UAE, as well the neighbouring country of Oman, all warrant exploration and there's plenty out there to keep you busy.

All six of the other emirates in the UAE – Ajman, Dubai, Fujairah, Ras Al Khaimah, Sharjah and Umm Al Quwain – are within a three-hour drive of central Abu Dhabi. From the sleepy streets of Umm Al Quwain and the rugged mountains of Ras Al Khaimah to the cultural grandiose of Sharjah, each emirate has something different to offer, and each can be explored, at least in part, over a weekend or on a day trip.

Dubai, in particular, should be visited if you have time – ideally for a weekend at least. The drive takes an hour or two, depending on which part of the capital you're leaving from and where in Dubai is your destination. Once there, you're surrounded by essential attractions to explore, from Burj Khalifa (the world's tallest building) and the delightful Dubai Marina (great for an evening stroll), to Mall of the Emirates (with its famous ski slopes), The Dubai Mall and Palm Jumeirah, which is now a must-visit destination in its own right. Plus, you'll find some giant concerts and major international sporting events taking place all throughout the winter months, with the Dubai Rugby Sevens

and Dubai World Cup the highlights of the sporting (and social) calendar.

The country's vast deserts and harsh-looking mountains are equally accessible, with a copy of the *UAE Off-Road Explorer*, and can be reached within a couple of hours, if you need to escape civilisation for a while. All of the big tour operators offer one to several day excursions into the mountains or desert, including accommodation that ranges from camping to five-star hotels.

There are also several incredible resort hideaways that combine comfortable lodgings with unique activities; these are well worth a weekend away, if you're planning on spending a week or two in the UAE.

Abu Dhabi's status as an international hub means it's easy to find quick, cheap flights to the neighbouring GCC countries of Oman, Saudi Arabia, Qatar, Bahrain and Kuwait, none of which are more than a 90-minute flight away.

All You Need To Know

In addition to handy visitors' guides like *Abu Dhabi Top 10* and *Abu Dhabi Mini Visitors' Guide*, Explorer publishes the fantastic *UAE Off-Road Explorer*, *Oman Off-Road Explorer* and the *Ultimate UAE Explorer* – if you love getting outdoors and active on your holidays, these guides contain everything you need to know. Pick up your copies online from askexplorer.com/shop.

Hatta

Web hattaforthotel.com
Tel 04 809 9333
Map 1 p.213

Less than an hour from Dubai, Hatta feels a whole world away, making it a great spot for a break from the hustle and bustle. Outside the town, there are plenty of off-roading opportunities, including the Hatta pools where you can take a cooling dip. If you prefer your action on two wheels, then this is also a popular area for cyclists.

Back in town, the Heritage Village is constructed around an old settlement and was restored in the style of a traditional mountain village. Hatta's history goes back over 3,000 years and the area includes a 200-year-old mosque and a fort, which is now used as a weaponry museum. Hatta Fort Hotel is a secluded retreat featuring 50 chalet-style suites which come with patios overlooking the Hajar Mountains and the tranquil gardens; the hotel also doubles as the area's main activity provider, with swimming pools, floodlit tennis courts, mini-golf and a driving range, as well as an archery range (instruction is available).

Oman

Web oman.com
Map 2 p.213

The most accessible country from the UAE, Oman is a peaceful and breathtaking destination, with history, culture and spectacular scenery to spare. The capital, Muscat, has enough attractions to keep you busy for a long weekend, with beautiful beaches, great restaurants and cafes, the mesmerising old souk at Mutrah, and the Sultan Qaboos Mosque.

Outside the capital are many historic towns and forts. You'll also discover some of the most stunning mountain and wadi scenery in the Middle East, with the region's highest peaks begging to be explored by hikers and mountain bikers. Salalah, in the south of Oman, has the added bonus of being cool and wet even during the summer months, which gives it a very different appearance to the rest of the Arabian Peninsula.

The drive from Abu Dhabi to Muscat takes just five hours, or you can hop on a flight from Abu Dhabi to Muscat which takes just an hour.

Dubai

Web dubai.ae **Map** 3 p.213

Cliches tend to trip off the tongue when describing Abu Dhabi's little brother – the city of gold, sleepy fishing village transformed into modern metropolis, the Vegas of the Middle East, and so on. The truth is that, while the emirate boasts an incredible number of attractions claiming to be the tallest, biggest or longest, it's not all bright lights – the atmospheric old town around the Creek, and the restored Bastakiya area are musts for any visitor wanting to scratch Dubai's cultural surface. The beautiful Jumeirah Mosque is one of the few mosques in the region open to non-Muslims, offering a rare chance to learn about the impact of Islam on the local people.

If it is bright lights you're after, then you'll find plenty in Dubai. From skiing on real snow at Ski Dubai and plunging through shark-infested waters at Aquaventure, to shopping till you drop at The Dubai Mall and surveying the city from the world's tallest building, Burj Khalifa, a weekend trip to Dubai promises an action-packed, once-in-a-lifetime break.

Beyond the city, the desert opens up further possibilities and many visitors choose to combine a city break with a couple of nights camping with a tour group, or relaxing at a luxury desert resort such as Al Maha Desert Resort & Spa or Bab Al Shams. The endless list of five-star hotels, restaurants, bars and clubs will ensure a well fed and watered stay, and luxury spas and clean beaches provide ample opportunities to relax while in Dubai.

> The Dubai Dolphinarium (dubaidolphinarium.ae) at Creekside Park is a perfect family day out. There are carnival-like shows featuring dolphins and seals, as well as an opportunity to swim with them. Plus, as it's indoors, the dolphinarium can be enjoyed during the summer months.

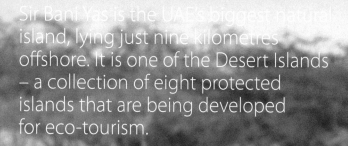

Sir Bani Yas is the UAE's biggest natural island, lying just nine kilometres offshore. It is one of the Desert Islands – a collection of eight protected islands that are being developed for eco-tourism.

It was the late Sheikh Zayed who turned Sir Bani Yas into Arabia's largest nature reserve as a way of protecting many natural species. The island plays a key role in conservation, with some 10,000 animals a year from Sir Bani Yas being released back into the wild.

04

Al Ain

Location 160km east of the capital, Abu Dhabi
Web abudhabi.ae **Map** 4 p.213

The capital of the eastern region and Abu Dhabi emirate's second city, Al Ain's greenery and the fact that it is the birthplace and childhood home of Sheikh Zayed bin Sultan Al Nahyan, the former (and much-loved) ruler of the UAE, gives it special status in the hearts and minds of Emiratis.

It takes an hour and a half by car to get there and most tour companies offer excursions to this fascinating 'Garden City' that straddles the border with Oman; the UAE side is known as Al Ain and the Oman side as Buraimi.

As a destination, Al Ain combines the old with the new. The city's archaeological legacy is of such significance that Al Ain is now a UNESCO World Heritage Site, with the 18 fortresses around the city and the seven natural oases all demanding exploration; the oasis palm plantations provide welcome shade and a haven from the city. On the outskirts of Al Ain, you will also find a Camel & Livestock Souk (adach. ae) which is worth a visit. Just outside the city, you'll find the mountain of Jebel Hafeet and Al Ain Zoo.

For those who like their thrills and spills, there's Wadi Adventure (p.43), karting at Al Ain Raceway (alainraceway.com), and rides for all the family at Hili Fun City (p.36).

05

The Pearl Coast

Location West of Abu Dhabi, from Mirfa to Jebel Dhanna
Map 5 p.212

The coastline that stretches west from Abu Dhabi towards the Saudi border is actually some of the least explored terrain by both tourists and residents – a shame as it's where you'll find charming towns and, most significantly, wide golden beaches with turquoise lagoons.

About 140km west of Abu Dhabi is Mirfa – a small, quiet coastal town with a long stretch of beach that is a kitesurfer's paradise. Many choose to pitch tents right on the beach, especially during the popular Al Gharbia Watersports Festival that takes place in March or April each year. The event is a weekend of fireworks, competitive kitesurfing, wakeboarding and kayaking. The

Mirfa Hotel (almarfapearlhotels.com) is a nice beach resort, with a couple of restaurants and bars to choose from, as well as a wide range of watersports on offer.

Located two hours west of Abu Dhabi, Jebel Dhanna is a great coastal getaway. With a sandy beach and clear, shallow sea, it is one of the region's best kept secrets.

There are two hotels here: the plush five-star Danat Jebel Dhanna Resort (danathotels.com) and the Dhafra Beach Hotel (danathotels.com). Jebel Dhanna is also a good base for boat trips out to some of the islands, such as Dalma Island, as well as the departure point for some incredible scuba diving adventures.

06

Liwa

Location Al Gharbia, Western Region
Map 6 p.212

If you love the great outdoors, you're simply going to love Liwa. Jump in a 4WD and prepare yourself for the most adventurous off-road driving the UAE has to offer, and some of its most incredible scenery. Liwa is located on the edge of the Empty Quarter (or Rub Al Khali) and is a must for any off-roader or adventurer during their time in the Middle East.

Stretching into Oman, Yemen and Saudi Arabia, the Empty Quarter is the biggest sand desert on the planet, and the sheer scale of the scenery and the size of the dunes, which rise to heights of over 300 metres, has to be seen to be believed.

The Liwa area is home to one of the largest oases on the Arabian Peninsula which stretches over 150 kilometres and provides a surprising

amount of greenery. While the main feature of Liwa is the desert, there are also several other attractions which are worth exploring along the way, including tiny villages, a fish farm and some recently renovated forts. They are all interesting places to poke around in for an idea of what life used to be like in this remote corner of the country.

To access the biggest dunes and witness spectacular sunrises, camping is the most practical accommodation option. However, if home comforts are a necessity, try the convenient Liwa Hotel (almafrapearlhotels.com) which sits on the edge of the desert or, alternatively, the stunning five-star Qasr Al Sarab Desert Resort by Anantara (p.110) on the edge of the Liwa crescent.

07
Fujairah

Location Nr The Gulf Of Oman **Web** fujairah.ae
Tel 09 222 2111 **Map** 7 p.213

A trip to the east coast is a must for any west coast tourist wanting a slower, more authentic slice of Emirati life. Made up of the emirate of Fujairah and several enclaves belonging to Sharjah, the villages along the east coast sit between the rugged Hajar Mountains and the gorgeous Gulf of Oman.

The real draw here is the landscape. The surrounding hillsides are dotted with ancient forts and watchtowers, which add an air of charm. Off the coast, the seas and coral reefs make a great spot for fishing, diving and watersports, and the wadis, forts, waterfalls and even natural hot springs are fun to explore.

Northern Emirates

Location Ajman, Ras Al Khaimah, Sharjah and Umm Al Quwain
Map 8 p.213

The Northern Emirates is the collective term given for Ajman, Ras Al Khaimah, Sharjah and Umm Al Quwain, which lie to the north of Dubai – and there's plenty to discover.

Sharjah is the UAE's cultural capital, with an eclectic mix of museums, heritage preservation and souks. The surrounding Buheirah Corniche is popular for evening strolls.

Umm Al Quwain is probably best known for Dreamland – the country's original waterpark with views over a beautiful lagoon and flamingos. For a quirky experience, you can stay in cabins or tents within Dreamland.

With the Hajar Mountains rising just behind the city, the Arabian Gulf and the desert, Ras Al Khaimah has possibly the best scenery of any emirate. The terrain begs to be explored by intrepid sorts, while the forts and museums are also well worth checking out.

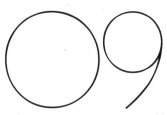

Emirates National Auto Museum

Location E65 Rd/Hamim Rd **Web** enam.ae
Tel 050 829 3952 **Times** 09:00-13:00, 14:00-18:00 (Daily)
Price Guide Dhs.10 **Map** 9 p.213

In spite of all the money that has been spent on big, bright attractions, occasionally in the UAE it is still possible to stumble upon something that is totally unexpected – and all the better for it. The Emirates National Auto Museum certainly falls into that category, providing something of a bizarre counterpoint to Yas Island's Ferrari World.

Located 45km south of Abu Dhabi, an impressive pyramid rises from the desert. Inside is an incredible assortment of cars belonging to one collector: Sheikh Hamad bin Hamdan Al Nahyan, aka the 'Rainbow Sheikh'. This includes the Sheikh's rainbow Mercedes collection.

Opened in 2005, the museum is now home to almost 200 cars, including a vast collection of off-road vehicles, classic American cars, and the largest truck in the world. Some exhibits were showcased in the BBC TV programme Top Gear.

Even if you're not particularly interested in cars, this is a fascinating collection and the globe caravan alone is worth the visit. The museum is ideal for an afternoon out of the city, or a pit stop on the journey to Liwa (p.212).

Al Maha Desert Resort & Spa

Location Dubailand **Web** al-maha.com
Tel 04 832 9900 **Map** 10 p.213

Calling Al Maha a hotel is a bit like calling the Rub Al Khali a bit of sand – this desert getaway is something else entirely and, if a few days here don't blow your mind, then we're not sure what will. Al Maha has been designed to resemble a typical Bedouin camp, but conditions are anything but basic. Each suite is beautifully crafted and has its own private pool and butler service.

There is a superb Timeless Spa on site, as well as The Terrace Bar and the excellent Al Diwaan restaurant, although most guests opt to have their meals served on their private decking – and why not? Especially when each room looks out on to the Dubai Desert Conservation Reserve with picturesque dunes, antelopes and Arabian red foxes to admire.

there's more to life...

The Region's Best Maps

ask**explorer**.com/shop

  /ask**explorer**

Maps

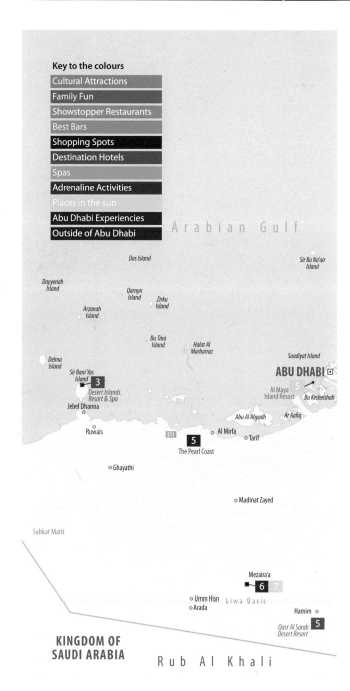

Key to the colours

- Cultural Attractions
- Family Fun
- Showstopper Restaurants
- Best Bars
- Shopping Spots
- Destination Hotels
- Spas
- Adrenaline Activities
- Places in the sun
- Abu Dhabi Experiencies
- Outside of Abu Dhabi

Arabian Gulf

Das Island

Sir Bu Na'air Island

Dayyenah Island

Qarnyn Island

Zirku Island

Arzanah Island

Bu Tina Island

Halat Al Marbarraz

Saadiyat Island

Delma Island

Sir Bani Yas Island **3**

Desert Islands Resort & Spa

Jebel Dhanna

ABU DHABI

Al Maya Island Resort **5**

Bu Kesheishah

Abu Al Abyadh

Ar Aafiq

Ruwais

E11

5

The Pearl Coast

Al Mirfa

Tarif

Ghayathi

Madinat Zayed

Sabkat Matti

Mezaira'a

6 **7**

Umm Hiṣn

Arada

Liwa Oasis

Hamim

Qasr Al Sarab Desert Resort **5**

KINGDOM OF SAUDI ARABIA

Rub Al Khali

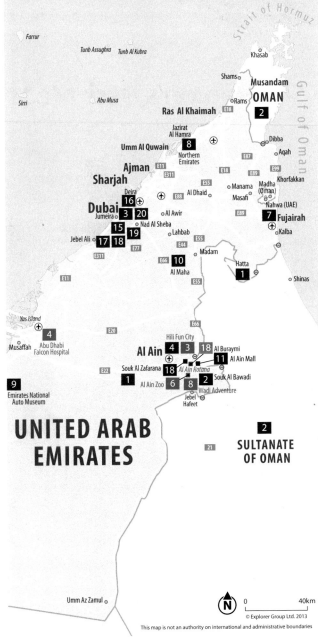

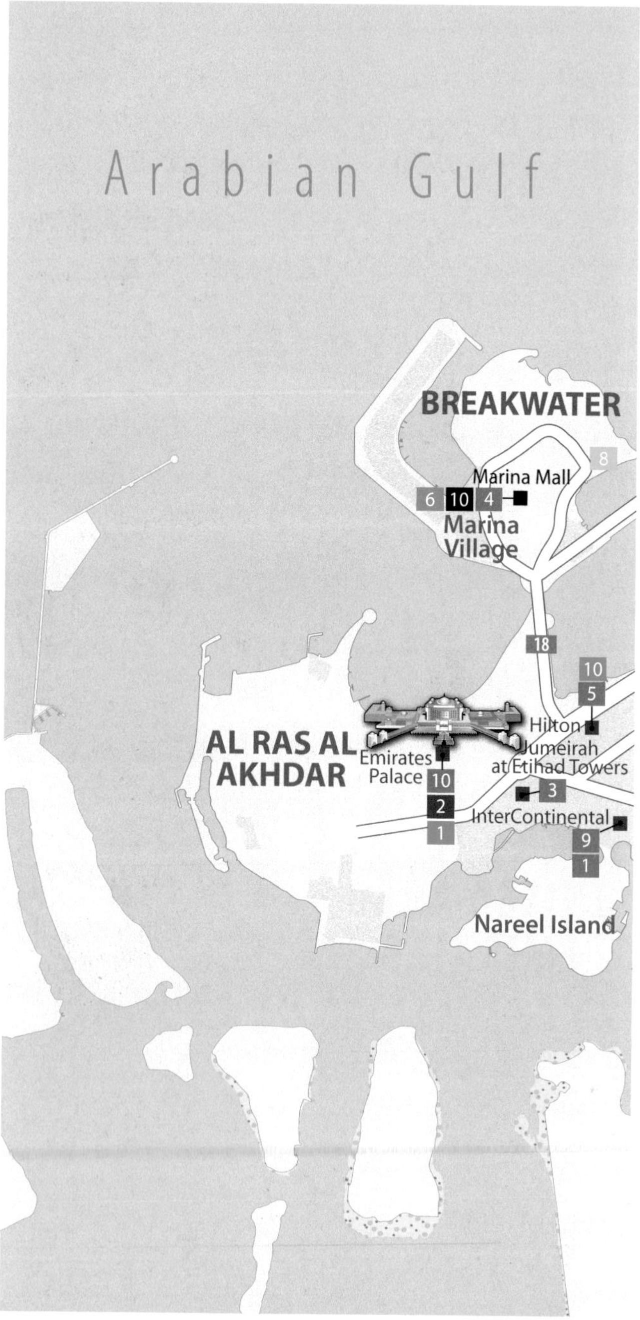

Arabian Gulf

BREAKWATER

Marina Mall

6 10 4

Marina
Village

8

18

10
5

AL RAS AL
AKHDAR

Emirates
Palace

Hilton
Jumeirah
at Etihad Towers

10
2
1

3

InterContinental

9
1

Nareel Island

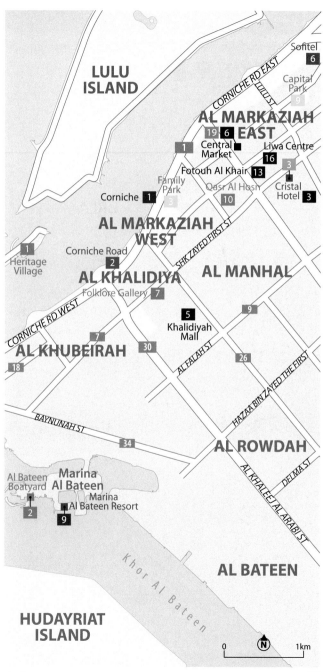

LULU ISLAND

CORNICHE RD EAST

Sofitel 6

LULU ST

Capital Park 9

AL MARKAZIAH EAST

19 6
Central Market

Liwa Centre

16

Fotouh Al Khair 13

3

Cristal Hotel 3

1

Corniche 1

Family Park 3

Qasr Al Hosn 10

AL MARKAZIAH WEST

Heritage Village 1

Corniche Road 2

SHK ZAYED FIRST ST

AL MANHAL

AL KHALIDIYA

Folklore Gallery 7

5
Khalidiyah Mall

9

CORNICHE RD WEST

7

30

26

AL KHUBEIRAH

18

AL FALAH ST

HAZAA BIN ZAYED THE FIRST

BAYNUNAH ST

34

AL ROWDAH

Al Bateen Boatyard

Marina Al Bateen

AL KHALEEJ AL ARABI ST

DELMA ST

2

Marina Al Bateen Resort

9

AL BATEEN

Khor Al Bateen

HUDAYRIAT ISLAND

0   N   1km

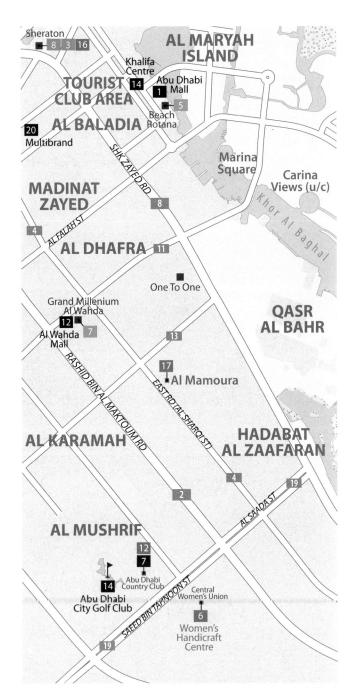

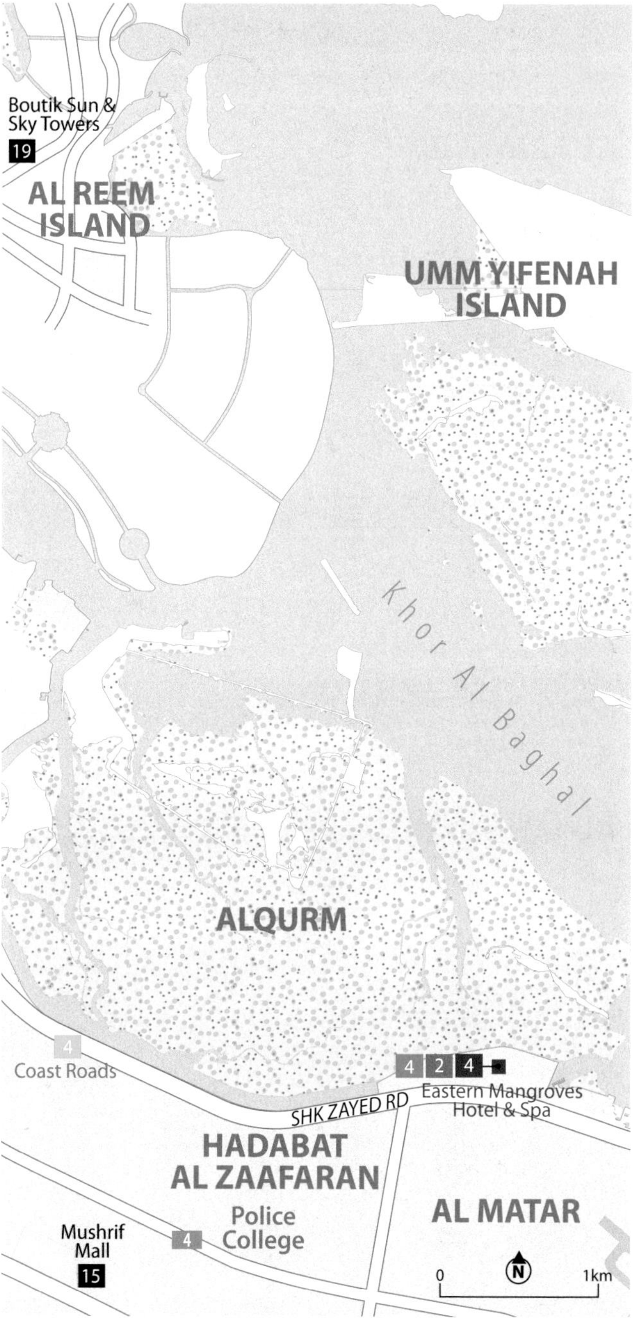

Boutik Sun &
Sky Towers

19

**AL REEM
ISLAND**

**UMM YIFENAH
ISLAND**

Khor Al Baghal

ALQURM

4

Coast Roads

4 **2** **4**

SHK ZAYED RD

Eastern Mangroves
Hotel & Spa

**HADABAT
AL ZAAFARAN**

AL MATAR

Mushrif
Mall

15

4

Police
College

0   (N)   1km

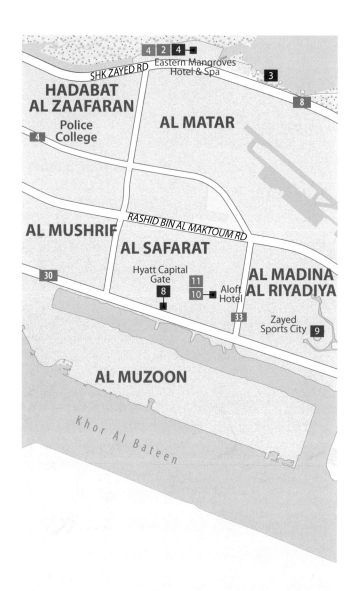

SHK ZAYED RD

Eastern Mangroves
Hotel & Spa

**HADABAT
AL ZAAFARAN**

Police
College

AL MATAR

RASHID BIN AL MAKTOUM RD

AL MUSHRIF

AL SAFARAT

Hyatt Capital
Gate

Aloft
Hotel

**AL MADINA
AL RIYADIYA**

Zayed
Sports City

AL MUZOON

Khor Al Bateen

HUDAYRIAT ISLAND

Abu Dhabi Top 10

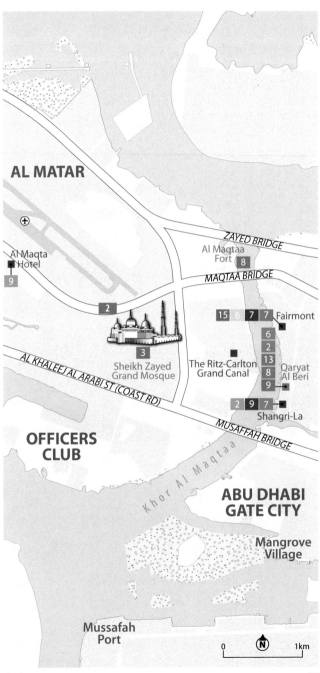

AL MATAR

ZAYED BRIDGE

Al Maqta Hotel
9

Al Maqtaa Fort **8**

MAQTAA BRIDGE

2

15 **6** **7** **7** Fairmont

6

2

3

13

Sheikh Zayed Grand Mosque

The Ritz-Carlton Grand Canal

8

9 Qaryat Al Beri

AL KHALEEJ AL ARABI ST (COAST RD)

2 **9** **7**

Shangri-La

MUSAFFAH BRIDGE

OFFICERS CLUB

Khor Al Maqtaa

ABU DHABI GATE CITY

Mangrove Village

Mussafah Port

0   **N**   1km

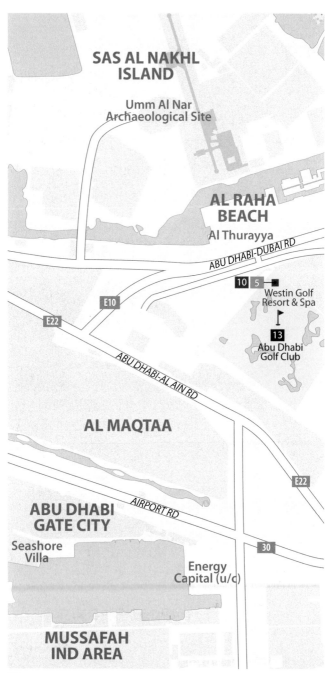

SAS AL NAKHL
ISLAND

Umm Al Nar
Archaeological Site

AL RAHA
BEACH

Al Thurayya

ABU DHABI-DUBAI RD

10 5

Westin Golf
Resort & Spa

E10

E22

13

Abu Dhabi
Golf Club

ABU DHABI-AL AIN RD

AL MAQTAA

E22

AIRPORT RD

ABU DHABI
GATE CITY

Seashore
Villa

30

Energy
Capital (u/c)

MUSSAFAH
IND AREA

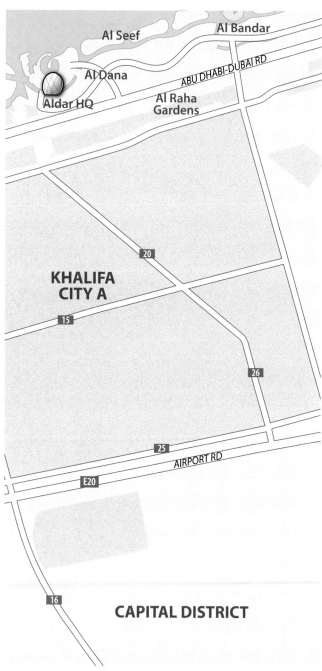

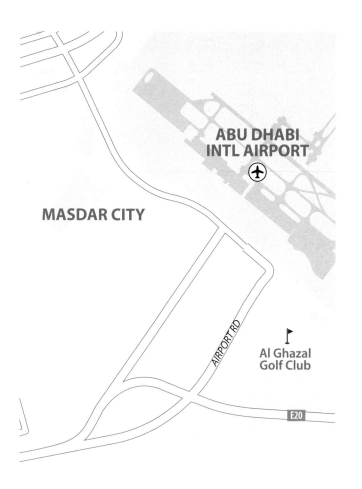

ABU DHABI INTL AIRPORT

MASDAR CITY

AIRPORT RD

Al Ghazal
Golf Club

E20

KHALIFA CITY B

0   N   1km

SHK KHALIFA HIGHWAY

YAS ISLAND WEST

4
5
Ferrari World

Yas Waterworld 7

12
Yas Links
Abu Dhabi

7

Yas Marina Circuit

8

20
9

4 1 1
Yas Yacht Club

Crowne Plaza
14
Yas Island Rotana
Yas Viceroy

AL QURAYYAH ISLAND

YAS ISLAND WEST

Khor Al Raha

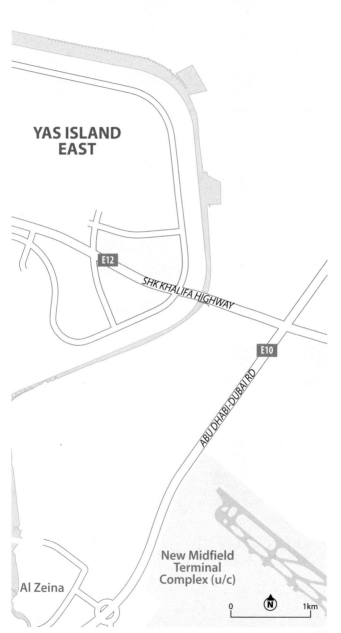

YAS ISLAND
EAST

E12

SHK KHALIFA HIGHWAY

E10

ABU DHABI-DUBAI RD

New Midfield
Terminal
Complex (u/c)

Al Zeina

0   N   1km

Arabian Gulf

SAADIYAT
CULTURAL
DISTRICT

AL MEENA

Fish, Fruit &
Vegetable Market
7

SHEIKH KHALIFA BRIDGE

Al Meena
Port
4

Iranian
8 Souk

E12

AL MEENA ST

Bainoona
Power Company

Central Business
District (u/c)

Arabian Gulf

10 6
Monte-Carlo
Beach Club

SAADIYAT
ISLAND

BAKE
Beach Park

2

Park Hyatt ■

11
Saadiyat Beach
Golf Club

8
■
St Regis

5
Manarat
Al Saadiyat

SHK KHALIFA HIGHWAY

SAADIYAT
ISLAND

Khor Laffan

0 ⊛ 1km
N

Index

A

Abaya 3
Abu Dhabi 1
Abu Dhabi Animal Shelter 37
Abu Dhabi Art Fair 23
Abu Dhabi Corniche 112, 159
Abu Dhabi Country Club 147
...ADVERT vii, 46
Abu Dhabi Desert Challenge 8
Abu Dhabi Falcon Hospital 37
Abu Dhabi Film Festival 8
Abu Dhabi International
Airport 4
Abu Dhabi Mall 87
Abu Dhabi Theatre 168
Abu Dhabi Tourism
Authority 101
Abu Dhabi Women's
Association 22
Accommodation 9
Adrenaline Activities 139
Agadir 119
Airport Transfer 4
Ajman 207
Al Ain 202
Al Ain Aerobatic Show 9
Al Ain Mall 93
Al Ain Zoo 40
...ADVERT iv
Al Bateen Boatyard 2, 17
Al Bateen Marina 150
Al Bateen Wharf 17
Al Dabayyah 146
Al Forsan International
Sports Resort 45
Al Gharbia Watersports
Festival 8, 203
Al Maha Desert Resort
& Spa 209
Al Maqta Hotel 10, 134
Al Maqtaa 113, 116
Al Maqtaa Fort 24
Al Maya 164
Al Meena 94
Al Meena Fruit and
Vegetable Souk 94
Al Meena Port 20, 95
Al Nahyan Family 1
Al Raha Beach Hotel 10
Al Wahda Mall 93
Alcohol 67
Aldar HQ 191
Ali Salem Edbowa 49, 63

Allure by Cipriani 79
Aloft Abu Dhabi 10, 81
Anantara Spa 106, 125
Arabian Divers &
Sportfishing 150
...ADVERT 151
Arabian Wildlife Park 106
Archery 45, 106
Architecture 190
Arts Abu Dhabi Gallery 21

B

BAKE 160
...ADVERT 154
Balloon Adventures 140
Bargaining 85
Bars 67
BAS Mall 96
Bawadi Mall 88
Bawadi Mall's Heritage
Village 88
Beach clubs 160, 165
Beach Rotana Abu Dhabi 130
Beachcomber 70
Beaches 157
Belly dancing 56
Birdwatching 109
Big Bus Tour 184
Bikinis 157
Boat Racing 183
Bord Eau 117
Bowling 44, 88
Boutique Sun & Sky Towers 93
Brazilian cuisine 61
Breakwater 16, 97, 168
Brunch 181
Bubbalicious Brunch 119
Bumper cars 44
Burj Al Marina 54
Bus 9
Bus tour 184

C

Cable park 45
Camel & Livestock Souk 202
Camel meat 63
Capital Park 169
Car Hire 9
Carpet Souk 95
Carrefour 90, 97
Caviar 77

Cedar Lounge 113
Central Market 93
Chamas Churrascaria & Bar 61
Champagne bars 71, 78
Championship Golf
Courses 188
CHI spa 126
Christmas 87
Cigar bar 74
Cinemas 31, 87, 88, 90, 91, 97
CityStore 97
Clay pigeon shooting 45
Climate 4
Cloud Nine 78
Club So-Hi 81
Cocktails 69
Contemporary Art Gallery 21
Corniche 7, 159, 168, 177
Corniche Beach 35
Corniche beach parks 157
Corniche Road 35
Crafts 22
Crime & Safety 6
Cristal Hotel Abu Dhabi 127
Cristal Spa 127
Crowne Plaza Yas Island 10
CuiScene 113
Cultural Attractions 15
Cultural Foundation 27
Culture 2
Currency 6
Cycling 9, 177

D

Dalma Mall 90
Debenhams 91
Desert 110, 139, 167
Desert driving 145
Desert hotels 101
Desert Islands Resort & Spa
by Anantara 10, 106
...ADVERT 107
Desert Safari 178
Dhow dinner cruise 186
Dhow harbour 20
Dhow racing 8, 183
Dhows 2
Diving 150
Dogs 157
Door policy 67
Dreamland 207
Driving 9

Dubai 199
Dubai Dolphinarium 199
...ADVERT 192
Dubai Dragon Boat Festival 183
Dune bashing 110, 145, 167

E

Eastern Mangroves Hotel &
  Spa by Anantara 51, 71, 108
Eastern Ringroad 163
Economy 3
Electricity & Water 4
Emirates National
  Auto Museum 208
Emirates Palace 10, 105, 125
Emirates Palace Marina 141
Emirates Park Zoo 32
...ADVERT 33
Emirati cuisine 63
Empty Quarter 110, 139, 205
ESPA 129
Events 8, 9

F

F1 concerts 185
Fairmont Bab
  Al Bahr 10, 49, 59, 113
Falcon Aviation Services 153
Falcons 37
Family Attractions 31
Family beaches 160
Family dining 59
Family Fun 31
Family Park 35, 161
Far Eastern cuisine 51
Ferrari World 39, 144
Fish Souk 94
Fishmarket 50
Flights 152
Folklore Gallery 23
Food & Drink 2
Football 44
Formal Park 35
Formula 1 39
Formula 1 Etihad Airways
  Abu Dhabi Grand Prix 9
Formula Rossa 39, 144
Forts 24, 27
Fotouh Al Khair 93
Frankie's 59
Fruit and Vegetable Souk 94
Fujairah 206

G

Gary Rhodes 49
Getting Around 9

Gold Souk 89
Golf 8, 119, 189
Golf courses 189
Grand Cinemas 96
Grand Millennium
  Al Wahda 132
Grand Mosque 18, 19

H

Hajar Mountains 195
Hammam 123
Hammour 50
Hatta 196
Hatta Fort Hotel 196
Hatta pools 196
Helicopter tours 153
Henna 22
Heritage Village 16, 196
Hili Fun City 36
...ADVERT 28
Hilton Abu Dhabi 10, 56, 135
Hiltonia Health Club & Spa 135
Home Centre 90
Hookah 182
Horse riding 45
Hot Air Balloon 140
Hotels 101
House of Fraser 93
Hubbly bubbly 182
Hummus 2
Hyatt Capital Gate 10, 114
...ADVERT 115

I

Ice rink 44
Iftar 49
Impressions 71
Indian cuisine 60
Indoor skydiving 147
InterContinental
  Abu Dhabi 10, 50
Internet 6
Iranian Souk 95
Iridium Spa 133
Islam 3
Italian cuisine 59, 63

J

Japanese 69
Jashanmal Bookstores
  ...ADVERT 12
Jebel Dhanna 203
Jumeirah At
  Etihad Towers 10, 52

K

Karting 45
Kayaking 43, 143
Khalidiyah Mall 91
Khalifa Centre 93
Khalifa Street Bridge 93
Kitesurfing 146

L

La Mer 112
Lake Park 35
Lamcy Plaza 93
Language 6
Le Deck 57
Lebanese 56
Left Bank 75
Lemon & Lime 74, 119
Liwa 110, 205
Liwa Centre 93
Louvre Abu Dhabi 15
LuLu hypermarket 89

M

Madinat Zayed Shopping
  Centre 89
Mall of the Emirates 93
Malls 93
Man/Age 131
Manarat Al Saadiyat 21
Manchester City 44
Marco Pierre White
  Steakhouse and Grill 58, 113
Marina Al Bateen Resort 150
Marina Mall 54, 97, 131, 168
Markaziya East 112
Mawal 56
Media 6
Men's spa 131
Mezlai 49, 63
Mezzaluna 63
Mezze 56
Mirage Marine 168
Mirfa Hotel 203
...ADVERT 64
Mizan 134
Mobile 6
Monte-Carlo
  Beach Club 57, 170
Motorsports 45
Mountain safari 167
Mubadala World Tennis
  Championship 9
Multibrand 93
Muscat 197
Mushrif Mall 93
Mussafah 90

N

National Dress   3
Nature reserve   106, 200
Nightlife   67
Northern Emirates   207
Noukhada Adventure
   Company   143

O

OffRoad Zone   167
Oil   2
Old Fort   27
Oman   197
One To One Hotel –
   The Village   10

P

Pachaylen   51
PADI   150
Paddle boarding   164
Paintballing   45
Pan-Asian   53
Park Hyatt Abu Dhabi
   Hotel & Villas   10
Parks   35, 157
Pearl Coast   203
Pearls & Caviar   76, 117
Picnics   36, 161
Pool parties   164
Port Zayed   20
Powerboat Racing   9
Public holidays   7

Q

Qaryat Al Beri   10, 25
Qasr Al Hosn   27
Qasr Al Sarab Desert Resort
   by Anantara   10, 110
   ...ADVERT   111
Quest   52

R

Racing   149
Radio   7
Rafting   43
Ramadan   15, 49
Ras Al Khaimah   207
Relax@12   81
Religion   3
Restaurants   49
Revolving restaurant   54
Rhodes 44   49
Ripe Market   93
Ritz-Carlton Grand Canal   10
Rollercoasters   39, 41, 144

Rooftop lounge   77
Rub Al Khali   110, 139
Rush   68

S

Saadiyat Island   21, 169, 170
Saadiyat Public Beach   160
Sas Al Nakhl Island   119
Seafood   50
Seawings   152
   ...ADVERT   172
Shangri-La Hotel   10, 76, 126
Shangri-La Qaryat
   Al Beri   117
Sharjah   207
Shawarma   2
Sheikh Zayed   18
Sheikh Zayed
   Grand Mosque   15, 18, 113
Sheraton Abu Dhabi Hotel
   & Resort   70, 78
Shisha   3, 182
Sho Cho   69
Shopping   85
Shopping Hours   85
Shopping malls   93
Sir Bani Yas Island   106, 200
Sky Flyer   36
Skydive Dubai   147
Skydiving   147
Skylite   68, 103
Sofitel   112
   ...ADVERT   98, 120
Souk Al Bawadi   88
Souk Al Megnas   96
Souk Al Zafarana   93
Souk at Qaryat Al Beri   25, 75
Souks   20
Spa by Anantara   10
Spacewalk   147
Sparky's Family Fun Centre   91
Spas   123
Spice Island   59
St Regis Saadiyat Island
   Resort   10, 133
Suhoor   49
Surf pool   43
Sushi   69

T

Taxi   9
Television   7
Tennis   44
Thai cuisine   51
Theme park   39
Tiara   54
   ...ADVERT   55

Time   4
Tourist Club Area   87
Trucial States   1

U

Umm Al Quwain   207
Universal Art Gallery   21
Urban Park   35
Useful Numbers   228
Ushna   60

V

Vegetarian dishes   61
Visas & Customs   4

W

Wadi Adventure   43
   ...ADVERT   136
Wafi   90, 93
Wakeboarding   45, 164
Walking & Cycling   9
Water & Electricity   4
Waterparks   41
Watersports   164
Weather   6
Westin Abu Dhabi Golf
   Resort & Spa   10, 74, 119
White Fort   27
White water rafting   43
Wildlife   40
WOMAD Abu Dhabi   8
Women's Handicraft
   Centre   22
World Trade Centre
   Abu Dhabi   93

Y

Yas Island   146, 149, 185
Yas Island West   103
Yas Marina Circuit   148
Yas Viceroy   10, 68, 103, 129
Yas Waterworld   41
Yas Yacht Club   79
Yellow Boats, The   141
Yotto   79

Z

Zayed National Museum   21
Zayed Sports City   44
Zayna Spa   132
Zen The Spa   130
Zoo   32

Notes

Notes

USEFUL NUMBERS

Embassies & Consulates

Australia	02 401 7500
Bahrain	02 665 7500
Canada	02 694 0300
Czech Republic (Embassy)	02 678 2800
China	02 443 4276
Egypt	02 813 7000
Finland	02 632 8927
France	02 813 1000
Germany	02 644 6693
India	02 449 2700
Iran	02 444 7618
Ireland	02 495 8200
Italy	02 443 5622
Japan	02 443 5696
Jordan	02 444 7100
Kuwait	02 447 7146
Lebanon	02 449 2100
Malaysia	02 448 2775
New Zealand	02 441 1222
The Netherlands	02 695 8000
Oman	02 446 3333
Pakistan	02 444 7800
Philippines	02 639 0006
Poland	02 446 5200
Qatar	02 449 3300
Russia	02 672 1797
Saudi Arabia	02 444 5700
South Africa	02 447 3446
Spain	02 626 9544
Sri Lanka	02 631 6444
Sweden	02 417 8800
Switzerland	02 627 4636
Syria	02 444 8768
Thailand	02 557 6551
UK	02 610 1100
USA	02 414 2200
Yemen	02 444 8457

Emergency Services

Abu Dhabi Police	999
Ambulance	999
Fire Department	997
AAA (Roadside Assistance)	800 8181

24-Hour Pharmacies

Sheikh Khalifa Medical City ER Pharmacy	02 819 2188
Lifeline Hospital Pharmacy	02 633 3340
Al Noor Hospital Pharmacy	02 613 9100
Al Ain Hospital Pharmacy	03 763 5888
Liwa Hospital Pharmacy	02 882 2204

A&E Departments

Al Ain Hospital	03 763 5888
Al Noor Hospital	02 626 5265
Al Rahba Hospital	02 506 4444
Al Salama Hospital	02 696 6777
Corniche Hospital	02 672 4900
Emirates International Hospital	03 763 7777
Hospital Franco-Emirien	02 626 5722
Madinat Zayed Hospital	02 884 4444
Mafraq Hospital	02 501 1111
National Hospital	02 671 1000
NMC Specialty Hospital	02 633 2255
Oasis Hospital	03 722 1251
Sheikh Khalifa Medical City	02 610 2000
Tawam Hospital	03 767 7444

Taxi Services

Al Ghazal Transport	02 444 7787
Al Ghazal Transport	03 751 6565
Arabia Taxi	800 272 242
CARS Taxi	800 227 789
National Taxi	600 543 322
Tawasul Transport	02 673 4444
Tawasul Transport	03 782 5553
TransAD	600 535 353

Airport Info

Etihad Airways	02 511 0000
Emirates Airline	600 55 55 55
Abu Dhabi International Airport Help Desk	02 505 5555
Flight Information	02 575 7500
Baggage Services	02 505 2771

Directory

Abu Dhabi Municipality	800 555
Abu Dhabi Police	02 699 9999
Al Ain Police	03 715 1100
UAE Country Code	+971
Abu Dhabi Area Code	02
Weather	02 666 7776
du Contact Centre (mobile enquiries)	
From mobile	155
From any UAE phone	800 155
du Contact Centre (home enquiries)	04 390 5555
Directory Enquiries (du)	199
Directory Enquiries (Etisalat)	181
Etisalat Customer Care	101
Mobile Phone Code (du)	052/055
Mobile Phone Code (Etisalat)	050/056
Speaking Clock	141
Traffic Police Dept	02 895 5111

BASIC ARABIC

General

Yes	*na'am*
No	*la*
Please	*min fadlak (m)*
	min fadliki (f)
Thank you	*shukran*
Please (in offering)	*tafaddal (m)*
	tafaddali (f)
Praise be to God	*al-hamdu l-illah*
God willing	*in shaa'a l-laah*

Greetings

Greeting (peace be upon you)	*as-salaamu alaykom*
Greeting (in reply)	*wa alaykom is salaam*
Good morning	*sabah il-khayr*
Good morning (in reply)	*sabah in-nuwr*
Good evening	*masa il-khayr*
Good evening (in reply)	*masa in-nuwr*
Hello	*marhaba*
Hello (in reply)	*marhabtayn*
How are you?	*kayf haalak (m)/*
	kayf haalik (f)
Fine, thank you	*zayn, shukran (m)/*
	zayna, shukran (f)
Welcome	*ahlan wa sahlan*
Welcome (in reply)	*ahlan fiyk (m) / ahlan fiyki (f)*
Goodbye	*ma is-salaama*

Introductions

My name is...	*ismiy…*
What is your name?	*shuw ismak (m)/*
	shuw ismik (f)
Where are you from?	
min wayn inta (m) / min wayn inti (f)	
I am from…	*anaa min...*
America	*ameriki*
Britain	*braitani*
Europe	*oropi*
India	*al hindi*

Questions

How many / much?	*kam?*
Where?	*wayn?*
When?	*mataa?*
Which?	*ayy?*
How?	*kayf?*
What?	*shuw?*
Why?	*laysh?*
Who?	*miyn?*
To/for	*ila*

In/at	*fee*
From	*min*
And	*wa*
Also	*kamaan*
There isn't	*maa fee*

Taxi Or Car Related

Is this the road to...	*hadaa al tariyq ila...*
Stop	*kuf*
Right	*yamiyn*
Left	*yassar*
Straight ahead	*siydaa*
North	*shamaal*
South	*januwb*
East	*sharq*
West	*garb*
Turning	*mafraq*
First	*awwal*
Second	*thaaniy*
Road	*tariyq*
Street	*shaaria*
Roundabout	*duwwaar*
Signals	*ishaara*
Close to	*qarib min*
Petrol station	*mahattat betrol*
Sea/beach	*il bahar*
Mountain/s	*jabal/jibaal*
Desert	*al sahraa*
Airport	*mataar*
Hotel	*funduq*
Restaurant	*mata'am*
Slow down	*schway schway*

Accidents & Emergencies

Police	*al shurtaa*
Permit/licence	*rukhsaa*
Accident	*haadith*
Papers	*waraq*
Insurance	*ta'miyn*
Sorry	*aasif (m) / aasifa (f)*

Numbers

Zero	*sifr*
One	*waahad*
Two	*ithnayn*
Three	*thalatha*
Four	*arba'a*
Five	*khamsa*
Six	*sitta*
Seven	*saba'a*
Eight	*thamaanya*
Nine	*tiss'a*
Ten	*ashara*
Hundred	*miya*
Thousand	*alf*

Explorer Products

Residents' Guides

Mini Visitors' Guides

Photography Books & Calendars

Check out ask**explorer**.com

Maps

Adventure & Lifestyle Guides

Abu Dhabi Top 10 – 1st Edition

Lead Editor Carli Allan
Editorial Team Matt Warnock, Stacey Siebritz, Lisa Crowther
Data Management Amapola Castillo
Sales Bryan Anes, Sabrina Ahmed
Design Ieyad Charaf, Jayde Fernandes
Maps Zain Madathil
Photography Henry Hilos, Ieyad Charaf, Pamela Grist, Pete Maloney, Victor Romero

Publishing
Founder & CEO Alistair MacKenzie
Associate Publisher Claire England

Editorial
Managing Editor – Consumer Carli Allan
Guides Editor Jo Iivonen
Deputy Guides Editor Stacey Siebritz
Managing Editor – Corporate Charlie Scott
Deputy Corporate Editor Lily Lawes
Digital Projects Editor Rachel McArthur
Web Editor Laura Coughlin
Production Assistant Vanessa Eguia
Editorial Assistant Amapola Castillo
Researchers Gayathri CM, Farida, Jagadeesh, Shalu M Sukumar, Suchitra P, Sreejith, Roja P

Design & Photography
Creative Director Pete Maloney
Art Director Ieyad Charaf
Designer Michael Estrada
Junior Designer M. Shakkeer
Layout Manager Jayde Fernandes
Cartography Manager Zainudheen Madathil
Cartographers Noushad Madathil, Dhanya Nellikkunnummal, Ramla Kambravan, Jithesh Kalathingal
GIS Analyst Rafi KM, Hidayath Razi
Photography Manager Pamela Grist
Photographer Bart Wojcinski
Image Library Jyothin

Sales & Marketing
Group Media Sales Manager Peter Saxby
Media Sales Area Managers Laura Zuffova, Sabrina Ahmed, Bryan Anes, Adam Smith, Louise Burton, Matthew Whitbread
Business Development Manager Pouneh Hafizi
Corporate Solutions Account Manager Vibeke Nurgberg
Group Marketing & PR Manager Lindsay West
Senior Marketing Executive Stuart L. Cunningham
Group Retail Sales Manager Ivan Rodrigues
Retail Sales Coordinator Michelle Mascarenhas
Retail Sales Area Supervisors Ahmed Mainodin, Firos Khan
Retail Sales Merchandisers Johny Mathew, Shan Kumar
Retail Sales Drivers Shabsir Madathil, Najumudeen K.I., Sujeer Khan
Warehouse Assistant Mohamed Haji

Finance, HR & Administration
Accountant Cherry Enriquez
Accounts Assistants Sunil Suvarna, Joy Bermejo Belza, Jeanette Carino Enecillo
Admin Assistant & Reception Joy H. San Buenaventura
Public Relations Officer Rafi Jamal
Office Assistant Shafeer Ahamed
Office Manager – India Jithesh Kalathingal

IT & Digital Solutions
Digital Solutions Manager Derrick Pereira
IT Manager R. Ajay
Database Programmer Pradeep T.P.

Contact Us

General Enquiries
We'd love to hear your thoughts and answer any questions you have about this book or any other Explorer product. Contact us at **info@askexplorer.com**

Careers
If you fancy yourself as an Explorer, send your CV (stating the position you're interested in) to **jobs@askexplorer.com**

Contract Publishing
For enquiries about Explorer's contract publishing arm and design services contact **contracts@askexplorer.com**

PR & Marketing
For PR and marketing enquiries contact **marketing@askexplorer.com**

Corporate Sales & Licensing
For bulk sales and customisation options, as well as licensing of this book or any Explorer product, contact **sales@askexplorer.com**

Advertising & Sponsorship
For advertising and sponsorship, contact **sales@askexplorer.com**

Explorer Publishing & Distribution
PO Box 34275, Dubai, United Arab Emirates
askexplorer.com

Phone: +971 (0)4 340 8805
Fax: +971 (0)4 340 8806